The Great Awakening
of the Black Hebrew Israelites…
in these last days

by

Jacqueline A. French

Cover Design: SOS Graphics

Edited by: Anthony Ambrogio

Published by G Publishing, LLC

ISBN: 978-0-9985990-1-4

Printed in the United States of America

Dedication

This book is dedicated to the Young Generation of Hebrew Israelites who are yet to come into the truth and knowledge of their true heritage and true ethnic identity as Hebrew Israelites, the bloodline descendants of the Biblical Israelites and physical seed of Abraham, Isaac, and Jacob. It will be with the coming of this Young Generation that the judicial blindness regarding their identity will be lifted to a major degree. These young "Joshuas" will need to prepare themselves mentally and spiritually for both the privilege and responsibility of leading their generation into this truth and to brace themselves for the perilous times that lie ahead.

Disclaimer

This book strictly focuses on awakening and tracing the identification of a People to its *Biblical* Hebrew Roots as the physical descendants of the **Hebrew Israelites** of the Bible and as the physical seed of Abraham, Isaac, and Jacob. It does not serve to endorse or advocate for organizations or camps that bear the same name. The book's Introduction fully clarifies its purpose and objectives.

Acknowledgments

I want to thank all who granted me permission to use their valuable quotes, materials, and information in this book. They added greatly to my success in accomplishing the book's objective.

Please note, however, that Permission for Use granted by these various and gifted individuals and/or use of certain information does not necessarily imply endorsement of the book's content or its objective. Nonetheless, the Right to agree or disagree is afforded to all, which makes the freedom of expression and speech that much more valuable and honored.

It is my hope that, upon careful and prayerful reading of this book, however, all doubters and/or objectors will be swayed to embrace the truths contained within its covers. By reading this book from its truest and purist perspective, one will see that the book is my heartfelt Love Letter to and from the Father, who inspired me in its writing, and to the World at large.

Lastly, I would like to acknowledge and give special thanks to my editor, Anthony Ambrogio, my book cover designer, Sharlean Muhammad of SOS Graphics, Shem chart designer, Myra Dillingham and my publisher, Julia Hunter of G Publishing LLC. You guys are the greatest!

Table of Contents

Illustrations

Introduction

Since the Nation of Israel (i.e. God's Chosen People) plays such an important role in Bible History, as well as in end-time prophecy, it behooves us to identify and know who the Nation or the Children of Israel are in the Bible and who they are today. The identification of any people, especially God's Chosen People, begins with God Himself. In His Word, God not only identifies exactly who His Chosen people are but also who and where they would be in the latter days, both physically and situationally. This book takes a biblical journey through the Holy Scriptures that reveals beyond doubt who God's Chosen ethnic people were and are today and is supported by archeological, historical, and genetic evidence, which the book will illustrate. In discerning the identification of God's Chosen People through scripture, it is important to keep the following foundational truths in mind: There is nothing new under the sun (Eccles. 1:9). God is the same today, yesterday and forever (Heb.13:8). God is a Spirit, and those that worship Him must Worship Him in Spirit and in Truth (John 4.24).

There is Nothing new under the sun. This is an important truth to keep in mind when one looks at the repetitive reason for Israel's past and present-day captivity (i.e. idolatry and/or failure to keep God laws, statutes and commandments) and the repetitive manner in which God dealt with them (using other nations as an instrument to carry out His punishment or judgment against them). The Most High allowed His Children to go into captivity until such time that they repented of their disobedience to Him and collectively RETURNED unto Him. Wherein He then restored them and allowed them to return to their land.

God is the same yesterday today and forever. This is a truth that is important to keep in mind when interpreting biblical prophecies and understanding that a particular prophecy in the Bible may pertain to both an immediate biblical fulfillment as well as to a latter or end-time fulfillment. This truth may also apply to Satan to a degree, as he seems not to change, being the author and father of all lies. He is a deceiver and the great deceiver of mankind. He leads people to believe a lie. He has people believing that light is dark and dark is light; that right is wrong and wrong is right; that good is evil and evil is good, and even has the world believing that Jews are Gentiles and *Gentiles* are Jews. However, those who know the truth yet perpetuate the lie are Servants of his kingdom that is doomed to fail.

God is a Spirit and those that worship Him must Worship Him in Spirit and in Truth. Worshiping God in Spirit and in truth does not just pertain to spiritual truth but to EVERY form of truth, including *historical* truth. Truth is truth, no matter where it is found. And, being truth, we know that it originates from God Himself, He being the Father and spirit of TRUTH. History then, or more specifically World History, is no more than HIS STORY being unveiled before man. Thus, God's Providential Hand is in everything that takes place in this world. *No worldly event happens by chance.* God's providence is seen throughout the world, and His Providential Hand is seen throughout world history as He causes one Nation to rise and another to fall; as He uses nations but as instruments in His hand to carry out His punishment or judgments against other nations, including Israel, even using them as a rod of correction against His Chosen People, the Children of Israel.

Using these foundational truths and additional scripture, it shall be unveiled to the reader the identity of God's chosen ethnic people—who they were and who they still are today. While the book uses the term *"Black* Hebrew Israelites" in its title, the unnecessary descriptor throughout the book has intentionally been dropped. Just as it is not necessary to describe a once-called "Negro" as a Black Negro or even a Caucasian as a White Caucasian, it is not necessary and is redundant to describe a Hebrew Israelite as a Black Hebrew Israelite. Scripture and archaeological evidence reveals them as "people of colour," as they were and currently are today. For this reason, the descriptor "Black" has been dropped and the proper or accurate name, Hebrew Israelites, is used in the book instead.

Though the book is primarily written to help awaken God's ethnic Chosen People—the Hebrew Israelites, to their true identity, it is also written to Hebrew Israelites who have already awakened unto their true identity but seem to be misguided in certain aspects of this revelation. However, while these are the primary targeted audiences, the book is ultimately written to anyone who seeks truth and will receive it.

As I am coming into the knowledge and truth of my heritage as a Hebrew Israelite, I may at times resort to Christian vernacular in addressing the Most High God and Jesus the Christ. Along this same line, I am aware of the ongoing debate even regarding the correct spelling of the Messiah's Hebrew name. Knowing this, I have nevertheless resigned myself to use one particular Hebrew spelling of His name throughout the book. More than trying to be politically correct, I am trying to present and convey truth. I hope the failure in the former does not overshadow the objective of the latter.

Also, realizing all of the problematic meanings, etymology/origin, and "coinage" of the very word "Jew"—that its historical reference originally applied to the inhabitants of Judea only (i.e. a Judean), then to the tribe of Judah, and later came to be applied to all twelve tribes of Israel in general—I use the terms Jew(s), Children or Nation of Israel, Israelites, and Hebrew Israelites interchangeably in the book to refer to the same group of people: God's Chosen People.

Finally, there may be many who will take issue with what is presented in this book. Many who may disagree and many who may even be greatly offended by its content. Be that as it may. In the final analysis it is *God's Word*, not man's arguments, that settles the matter on any issue or question at hand. On this, I'm sure we can all agree. Now that I have said this, let us begin our biblical journey into truth.

(Note: All scripture quotations in the book are taken from the King James Version of the Holy Bible.)

Chapter One:
The Great Awakening

As mentioned in the Introduction, the identification of any people, especially God's Chosen people, begins with God himself. Not with any noted historian or theologian; not with an "expert" in whatever field void of scriptural truth— but with God. Thus, through scripture, God Himself identifies who his Chosen People were, who they are today, and where they would be in the last days both physically and situationally. So prepare as we begin our biblical journey through the Holy Scriptures and see what truths unfold regarding God's Chosen People—who they were and who they still are today. We begin with scriptures that clearly identify God's Chosen People as being the Children or the Nation of Israel.

> *For thou art an holy people unto the LORD thy God: the LORD thy God hath chosen thee to be a special people unto himself, above all people that are upon the face of the earth.* (Deut. 7:6)

> *For thou art an holy people unto the LORD thy God, and the LORD hath chosen thee to be a peculiar people unto himself, above all the nations that are upon the earth.* (Deut.14:2)

> *When the Most High divided to the nations their inheritance, when he separated the sons*

[1]

of Adam, he set the bounds of the people according to the number of the children of Israel. For <u>the LORD's portion is his people; Jacob is the lot of his inheritance.</u> (Deut. 32:8-9; emphasis added)

And what one nation in the earth <u>is like thy people, even like Israel,</u> whom God went to redeem for a people to himself, and to make him a name, and to do for you great things and terrible, for thy land, before thy people, which thou redeemedst to thee from Egypt, from the nations and their gods? <u>For thou hast confirmed to thyself thy people Israel to be a people unto thee for ever;</u> and thou, LORD, art become their God. (2 Sam. 7:23-24; emphasis added)

For thou didst separate them from among all the people of the earth, **<u>to be thine inheritance,</u>** *as thou spakest by the hand of Moses thy servant, when thou broughtest our fathers out of Egypt, O Lord GOD.* (1Kings 8:53; emphasis added)

O LORD, there is none like thee, neither is there any God beside thee, according to all that we have heard with our ears. <u>And what one nation in the earth is like thy people Israel,</u> whom God went to redeem to be his own people, to make thee a name of greatness and terribleness, by driving out nations from before thy people, whom thou hast redeemed out of Egypt? (1 Chron. 17:20-21; emphasis added)

O ye seed of Abraham his servant, <u>ye children of Jacob his chosen.</u> (Ps.105:6; emphasis added)

For the LORD hath chosen <u>Jacob unto himself</u> <u>and Israel</u> for his peculiar treasure. (Ps. 135:4; emphasis added)

But thou, Israel, art my servant, Jacob <u>whom I</u> <u>have chosen</u>, the seed of Abraham my friend. Thou whom I have taken from the ends of the earth, and called thee from the chief men thereof, and said unto thee, <u>Thou art my</u> <u>servant;</u> I have chosen thee, and not cast thee away. (Isa. 41:8-9; emphasis added)

<u>Remember these, O Jacob and Israel; for thou</u> <u>art my servant:</u> I have formed thee; <u>thou art</u> <u>my servant:</u> O Israel, thou shalt not be <u>forgotten of me</u>. (Isa. 44:21; emphasis added)

Hearken unto me, O Jacob and Israel, my called; I am he; I am the first, I also am the last. (Isa. 48:12).

These scriptures verify beyond doubt that the Children of Israel were God's Chosen People. However, it is also necessary to *specifically* identify who the *Children* of Israel were so that it can be determined who they are today.

According to scripture, Noah had three sons, Shem, Ham and Japheth, and of them was the whole Earth overspread (Gen. 9:18-19). Abraham, the patriarch of Israel, was of the lineage of Noah's son Shem who was the progenitor of the Semitic ("Jewish") race. Abraham later had a son named Isaac, who in turn had a son named Jacob. Jacob, whose name God changed to Israel (Gen. 35:10) had twelve sons: Ruben, Simeon, Levi, Judah, Dan, Naphtali, Gad, Asher, Issachar, Zebulun, Joseph, and Benjamin. These twelve sons of Jacob made up

[3]

the Twelve Tribes or the Nation of Israel, also known as the Children of Israel, the House of Jacob, the Israelites, or simply, God's Chosen People. All descendants of Jacob's twelve sons were likewise Israelites and belonged to the Nation of Israel. This would include all past, *present*, and future descendants of Jacob's sons. Thus, in order to be a true Israelite or a natural Jew, one has to be a *physical* descendant of the biblical Israelites. That is, *one has to be a bloodline descendant* of one of Jacob's twelve sons in order to be a natural Jew or an Israelite.

The *European or Ashkenazi* "Jews" that are occupying the land of Israel today *are not* natural Jews. That is, they are *not* the physical or bloodline descendants of Abraham, Isaac, and Jacob through the lineage of Shem—the progenitor of the Semitic race. According to scripture, they are descendants of Noah's son Japheth—not Shem (Gen. 10:1-3). Therefore, they are not bloodline descendants of the ancient Israelites or Jews of the Bible with whom God made an everlasting covenant and promise. They are descendants of Japheth, who is the progenitor of the Indo-European race. The Bible additionally refers to Japheth's descendants as Gentiles (Gen. 10:1-5). *Therefore, as descendants of Noah's son Japheth and **not Shem**, the European/Ashkenazi "Jews" scripturally, are not Semitic or physical Jews at all. Rather they are Gentiles.*

Even modern DNA testing has shown that the European or Ashkenazi "Jews" are not bloodline descendants of Abraham, Isaac, and Jacob. The reader is encouraged to seek and do further research on this topic. Suggested resources include "The Missing Link of Jewish European Ancestry: Contrasting the Rhineland and the Khazarian Hypotheses" by E. Elhaik; *DNA Science and the Jewish Bloodline* by Texe Marrs; "Forbidden Knowledge: History of the Khazar Empire," a lecture by Jack Otto; and "Fake Jews and the Coming Destruction of Israel"—all which can be accessed online and whose links have been provided in the Suggested Resources section of this book.

Furthermore, "Jews" admit in their own writings that they are not the descendants of the ancient Jews/Israelites of the Bible. For instance, under the heading, "A Brief History of the Terms for Jew," the 1980 *Jewish Almanac* notes the following: "*Strictly* speaking, it is *incorrect* to call an ancient Israelite a 'Jew' or to call *a contemporary Jew an Israelite or a Hebrew*" (3; emphasis added). In addition, the *Jewish Encyclopedia (1901)* records the following with respect to *the origin* of the European or Khazar Jews:

> Chazars [Khazars]: A people of **Turkish** origin whose life and history are interwoven with the very beginnings of the history of the Jews of Russia. The Kingdom of the Chazars was firmly established in most of **South Russia** long before the foundation of the Russian monarchy by the Varangians (855). Jews lived on the shores of the Black and Caspian seas since the first centuries of the common era [after the death of Christ]. Historical evidence

[5]

points to the region of the Ural as the home of the Chazars. Among the classical writers of the Middle Ages they were known as the "Chozars," "Khazirs," "Akatzirs," and "Akatirs," in the Russian chronicles as "Khwalisses" and "Ugry Byelyye." (Emphasis added)

Also, the Encyclopedia Americana 1985 notes the following:

Khazar: *an ancient Turkic-speaking people* who ruled a large and powerful state in the steppes North of the ***Caucasus Mountains*** from the 7th century to their demise in the mid-11th century AD... In the 8th century, its political and religious head as well as the greater part of the Khazar nobility, abandoned paganism and converted to Judaism... (the Khazars are believed to be *the ancestors of most Russian and European Jews).* (Emphasis added)

Ashkenazim: the Ashkenazim are the Jews whose ***ancestors lived in German lands...*** it was among the *Ashkenazi [Khazar] Jews* that the idea *of political Zionism emerged,* leading ultimately to the establishment of the state of Israel... In the late 1960s, Ashkenazi Jews numbered some 11 million, *about 84 percent of the world Jewish population.* (Emphasis added)

Similarly, incontrovertible facts regarding the history and origin of European/Ashekenazi Jews can also be found in the following resources: *The Encyclopedia Judaica* (1971); *The Universal Jewish Encyclopedia;* the *New Encyclopedia Britannica*

[6]

(15th edition); *Academic American Encyclopedia* (1985) and the Holy Bible.

Credible resources even include Jewish authors themselves, such as Arthur Koestler, who wrote the 1976 best seller, *The Thirteenth Tribe* and Alfred M. Lilienthal. In his book, *The Zionist Connection II,* Lilienthal relates the following:

> ... The existence of [the State of] Israel is not founded on logic. It has no ordinary legitimacy. There is neither in its establishment nor present scope any evident justice—though there may be an utter need and wondrous fulfillment.'... In his 1976 best seller *The Thirteenth Tribe* [Arthur Koestler]... dropped another bombshell by proving that *today's Jews* were, for the most part, *descendants of Khazars, who converted to Judaism* seven centuries after the destruction of Jerusalem in 70 AD... Therefore **the great majority of Eastern European Jews are not Semitic Jews at all,** *and as most Western European Jews came from East Europe,* most of them are also *not Semitic Jews....* (759-768; emphasis added)

Finally, in his book, *Facts are Facts,* Benjamin Freedman, a self-proclaimed Jewish defector, relayed the following:

> ...You will probably be astonished as [many] Christians were years ago when I electrified the nation with the first publication by me of the facts disclosed by my many years of research into the origin and the history of the 'Jews' in Eastern Europe. My many years of intensive research established beyond the

[7]

question of any doubt, contrary to the generally accepted belief held by Christians, that the 'Jews' in Eastern Europe at any time in their history in Eastern Europe were ever the legendary 'lost ten tribes' of Bible lore. That historic fact is incontrovertible.

Relentless research established as equally true that the 'Jews' in Eastern Europe at no time in their history could be correctly regarded as the direct lineal descendants of the legendary 'lost ten tribes' of Bible lore. The 'Jews' in Eastern Europe **in modern history** cannot legitimately point to a single ancient ancestor who ever set even a foot on the soil of Palestine in the era of Bible history. Research also revealed that the 'Jews' in Eastern Europe *were never 'Semites,' are not 'Semites' now, nor can they ever be regarded as 'Semites' at any future time* by any stretch of the imagination. *Exhaustive research also irrevocably rejects as a fantastic fabrication the generally accepted belief by Christians that the 'Jews' in Eastern Europe are the legendary "Chosen People" so very vocally publicized by the Christian clergy from their pulpits.* (50; emphasis added)

These resources show that, historically, European Jews occupying the land of Israel today *are not* returning to their homeland of Israel or Palestine because they were never there in the first place. Their homeland is in the Caucasus region between the Black and Caspian seas of Eurasia, as noted by many historians. This is perhaps why technically they refer to themselves as Israelis and not Israelites. By definition, an *Israeli* is an occupant or resident of Israel. An *Israelite* is a

[8]

bloodline descendant of Abraham, Isaac, and Jacob, which they are not. It is also why, "Strictly speaking it is incorrect to call an ancient Israelite a 'Jew' *or to call a contemporary Jew an Israelite or a Hebrew*"—because they are not. Their very presence in the land of Israel today, however, does give credence to the scriptures found in Revelation 2:9 and 3:9:

> *I know your works, and tribulation, and poverty, (but you are rich) and I know the blasphemy of them who say they are Jews, and are not, but are the synagogue of Satan.* (Rev. 2:9; emphasis added)

> *Behold, I will make them of the synagogue of Satan, which say they are Jews, and are not, but do lie; behold, I will make them to come and worship before thy feet, and to know that I have loved thee.* (Rev. 3:9; emphasis added)

The European Jews' presence in the land of Jerusalem is also a fulfillment of the prophecy spoken by Jesus/Yehoshua Himself ". . . *and Jerusalem shall be trodden down of the Gentiles, until the times of the Gentiles be fulfilled*" (Luke 21:24). *The times of the Gentiles* refers to the period of Gentile domination over Israel. The period of Gentile domination was represented in King Nebuchadnezzar's vision of a giant statue recorded in the Book of Daniel ("What are times"). The first Gentile rule over Israel was Babylon, followed by Media-Persia, then Greece, followed by Rome. In the last days, the last Gentile rule (which is believed to be the "revised" Roman Empire) will be destroyed by Christ Himself (Dan. 2:24-44).

In Genesis, the Most High God made the following covenant with Abraham, "*And I will give unto thee, and to thy seed after thee, the land wherein thou art a stranger, all the land of Canaan, for an everlasting possession; and I will be their God*" (Gen. 17: 8; emphasis added). When GOD appeared to Jacob in Bethel, He renewed the covenant. He promised to give Jacob *and his descendants* the land of Canaan as an *everlasting possession* (Gen. 28:10-13; Gen. 35:10-12; Gen. 48:3-4). Thus, it was to Jacob and *his bloodline descendants* to whom God made the everlasting covenant. This, again, includes Jacob's past, *present-day*, and future bloodline descendants. Therefore, it is to Jacob and his natural descendants to whom God promised to give the Land of Canaan. We know that God will fulfill every promise that He has ever made, for scripture tells us that He is not a man that he should lie (Num. 23:19). We also know that He changes not and His promises are yea and Amen (2 Cor. 1:20).

A question that one must now ask is this: If the European Jews who are currently in the land of Israel *are not* the true Jews or bloodline descendants of Abraham Isaac, and Jacob, then who and where are the true Jews or bloodline descendants of the biblical Israelites with whom God made an everlasting covenant? We, again, turn to the scriptures for the answer. Scripture, unequivocally, identifies for us who the true Jews/Israelites are and where they are today.

Interestingly, the Bible tells us that, "*Truth shall spring out of the earth; and righteousness shall look*

[10]

down from heaven (Ps. 85:11; emphasis added); and, so it is. Out of the Earth, through archeological findings, springs truth about the physical appearance of the Ancient Egyptians as well as the physical appearance of the ancient Hebrew Israelites they enslaved.

It has been said that part of determining who a people are is establishing what they look like. Archeological evidence has shown the world that the Ancient Egyptians were a black or a dark race of people (who, by the way, were descendants of Ham: Gen. 10:6-20). The ancient Jews or Hebrew Israelites of the Bible physically resembled the Ancient Egyptians, who again were a black or a dark race of people. Thus, the Ancient Egyptians and Jews/Hebrew Israelites had the same skin coloring, which is why it was easy for the following *Jews in the Bible* to be *mistaken for Egyptians*: **Moses** (Exod. 2:15-21); **Joseph** (Gen. 42:3-8) and **Paul** (Acts 21:37-39).

After Jesus/Yehoshua was born, the Lord told Joseph to take him and his mother and flee to Egypt. Jesus/Yehoshua (in human flesh) and his earthly parents were Jews, being of the Tribe of Judah. If Jesus/Yehoshua, Mary, and Joseph were not of the same skin coloring as the ancient Egyptians, how could they abide or hide safely in Egypt until the death of King Herod (Matt 2:13-14)? Egyptians' paintings *of themselves* and of the Hebrews they enslaved are quite telling: the Egyptians depicted themselves and the Hebrews they enslaved as black or dark-skinned people on the walls of their pyramids/temples. Images below

[11]

show how Egyptians depicted themselves and their Hebrew slaves, as well as how they depicted Japhetic peoples.

Additional resource links have been provided in the Suggested Resources section for the reader who wishes to do further research into the physical similarities of the Ancient Hebrew Israelites and the Ancient Egyptians. Also, one can simply do an online search of "Images of Ancient Egyptians" and "Images of Ancient Hebrews" and see the telling images that appear.

Ancient Egyptian Men

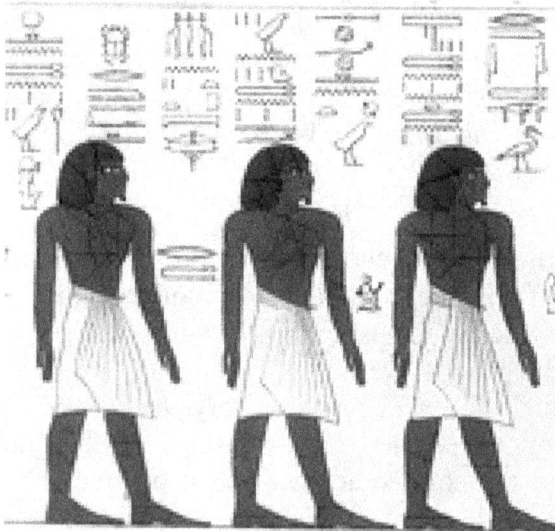

Figure 1: File: Giovanni Battista Belzoni: Egyptian race portrayed in the Book of Gates.jpg. (Modified/Cropped from original file). {{PD-Art|PD-old-70|PD-because|The original file is a faithful photographic reproduction of a two-dimensional public domain work of art. This photographic reproduction image is therefore considered to be in the public domain in the United States.}}

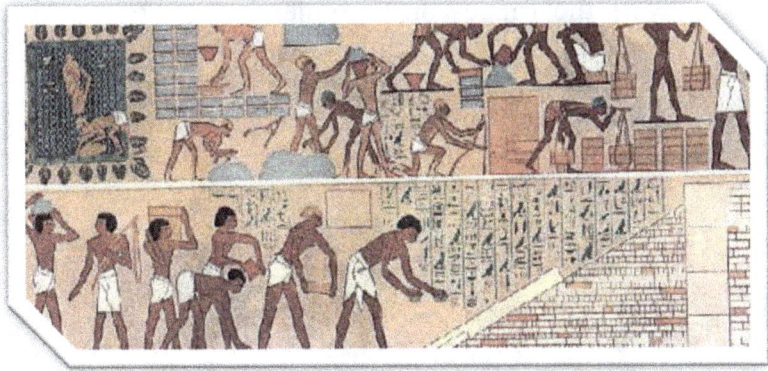

Figure 2a: File: Original Source- Illustrerad Verldshistoria band I III 04 jpg Egyptian prisoners at slavery from a wall painting in a grave at Thebes by Ernst Wallis et al, created 31 December 1875-9. Public-domain image (Modern/modified from original).

Regarding Hebrew Israelites as slaves in Egypt, scripture records, *"And they [the Egyptians] made their lives bitter with hard bondage, in mortar, and in brick, and in all manner of service in the field: all their service, wherein they made them serve, was with rigor"* (Ex 1:14).

Figure 2b: File: Figurine from Egypt of semitic slave (2) jpg. Author/ Owner Hanay 23 Mar..2013 CC BY-SA 3.0.

[13]

Note the fringes on the outer borders of their garments. Hebrew Israelites were commanded to wear fringes on their outer garments to remind them of God's commandments and do them (Num.15:37-41; Deut.22:12; "Images").

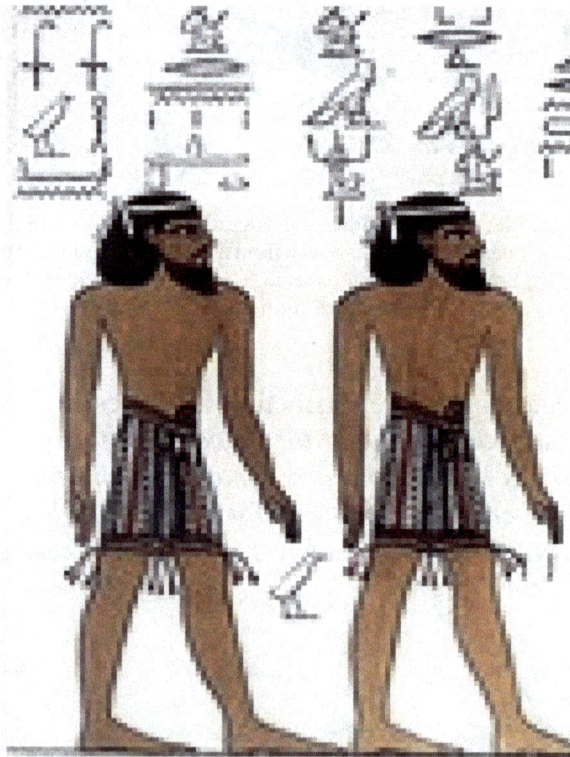

Figure 3: File Giovanni Battista Belzoni-Egyptian race portrayed in the Books of Gates. jpg Modified/Cropped from original file). {{PD-Art|PD-old-70|PD-because|The original file is a faithful photographic reproduction of a two-dimensional public domain work of art. This photographic reproduction image is therefore considered to be in the public domain in the United States.}}

Here is how the Ancient Egyptians depicted Japhetic (or **non**-Semitic/Hamitic) people. Notice the tattoos on their arms and legs as many of his descendants (Indo-Europeans) have today ("Images")

Figure 4. File: Giovanni Battista Belzoni-Egyptian race portrayed in the Books of Gates. jpg, (Modified/Cropped from original file). {{PD-Art|PD-old-70|PD-because|The original file is a faithful photographic reproduction of a two-dimensional public domain work of art. This photographic reproduction image is therefore considered to be in the public domain in the United States.}}

Thus, both scriptural and archeological evidence have shown that the original Hebrew Israelites/Jews of the Bible (i.e. God's Chosen People) were Black or people of color, and they still are today. Let us look once again at scripture to verify this fact.

Before we begin, however, let me reiterate this. God's Providential Hand is in everything that takes place in this world. No worldly event happens by chance, as World History is no more than His Story being unveiled on Earth. His Providential Hand is seen throughout history as it is He who causes a nation to rise and another to fall according to His set time (Acts 17:26). He is the same yesterday, today, and forever, and there is nothing new under the sun (Heb. 13:8; Eccles. 1:9).

The truth of these scriptures is readily apparent when we look at the history of God's Chosen People and the repetitive reason and manner in which He had to deal with them. *"Now therefore, if ye will obey my voice indeed, and keep my covenant, then ye shall be a peculiar treasure unto me above all people: And Ye shall be unto me a kingdom of priests and a holy nation..."* (Exod. 19:5-6). In response to God's Covenant, the Children of Israel whole-heartedly said, *"All that the Lord has spoken we will do,"* (Exod. 19:8). However, they failed miserably at this, time and time again.

Throughout scripture, we see how God used other nations as instruments of judgments against them each time they fell into idolatry or failed to keep His commandments. We have the Assyrian captivity of the Northern Kingdom (1 Chron. 5:26; 2 Kings 17:23; 2 Kings 18:11-12), the Babylonian Captivity of the Southern Kingdom (Ezra 5:12; Ezek. 17:12; 1 Chron. 9:1), and now Israel's present-day captivity or exile. It was the Israelites' idolatry and their failure to keep God's commandments that resulted in their bible-day captivities. It was also idolatry and failure to keep His commandments on the part of the Israelites' forefathers that has resulted in their present-day captivity. All as He had forewarned.

Interestingly, there are at least four scriptures that seem to prophetically point to a latter-day or end-time *captivity in a foreign and distant land* for the Children of Israel. For instance, upon their deliverance after 400 years of Egyptian bondage, Moses sang the following song:

> *Give ear, O ye heavens, and I will speak; and hear, O earth, the words of my mouth... For the LORD's portion is his people; Jacob is the lot of his inheritance. ... So the LORD alone did lead him, and there was no strange god with him... They provoked him to jealousy with strange gods, with abominations provoked they him to anger. They sacrificed unto devils, not to God; to gods whom they knew not, to new gods that came newly up, whom your fathers feared not... And he said, I will hide my face from them, I will see what their end shall be: for they are a very froward generation, children in whom is no faith. They have moved me to jealousy with that which is not God; they have provoked me to anger with their vanities: and I will move them to jealousy with those*

[17]

*which are not a people; I will provoke them to anger with a foolish nation. For a fire is kindled in mine anger, and shall burn unto the lowest hell, and shall consume the earth with her increase, and set on fire the foundations of the mountains I will heap mischiefs upon them; I will spend mine arrows upon them. They shall be burnt with hunger, and devoured with burning heat, and with bitter destruction: I will also send the teeth of beasts upon them, with the poison of serpents of the dust. The sword without, and terror within, shall destroy both the young man and the virgin, the suckling also with the man of gray hairs, I said, **I would scatter them into corners, I would make the remembrance of them to cease from among men**.* (Duet. 32:1, 9-26; emphasis added)

Remember, Moses sang this song *immediately following* the Children of Israel's miraculous deliverance from the Egyptians through the Red Sea by the mighty hand of God. So why would Moses *at this point* sing a song about the Lord's anger being kindled against the Children of Israel and God being provoked to deliver them over to a *"foolish nation"* which *"are not a people"*? While the song may be speaking prophetically of the subsequent Assyrian and Babylonian Captivities for the Northern and the Southern Kingdoms, respectively, it may also be speaking of the Children of Israel's present-day captivity or exile as well. Interestingly, the song declares that God would *scatter them into corners* and *make the remembrance of them to cease from among men.* This is characteristic of the Children of Israel today in their present-day captivity. Yet and

[18]

still, the song also foretells of a future restoration for God's people, following their ordained scattering and seeming "abandonment" by God:

> *To me belongeth vengeance, and recompence;* <u>*their foot shall slide in due time: for the day of*</u> <u>*their calamity is at hand*</u>, *and the things that shall come upon them make haste.* <u>*For the*</u> <u>*LORD shall judge his people, and repent*</u> <u>*himself for his servants,*</u> **when he seeth that** **their power is gone,** *and there is none shut up, or left.... Rejoice, O ye nations,* <u>*with his people*</u> <u>*for he will avenge the*</u> <u>*blood of his servants,*</u> <u>*and will render vengeance to his adversaries*</u> *and* <u>*will be merciful to his land*</u> <u>*and to his*</u> <u>*people.*</u> *(Deut. 32:35-36, 43; emphasis added)*

While again, the song may pertain to the Children of Israel's eventual Assyrian and Babylonian captivities, it may certainly pertain to their present day captivity as well. It is also interesting to note that triumphant saints of the end-time tribulation will too, sing the Song of Moses (Rev. 15:3-4).

The prayer prayed by King Solomon during the dedication of the Temple is another scripture that seems to prophetically point to a latter or end-time captivity for the Children of Israel *in a foreign and distant land*. Note the prayer below:

> *And he said, LORD God of Israel, there is no God like thee, in heaven above, or on earth beneath, who keepest covenant and mercy with thy servants that walk before thee with all their heart.... And hearken thou to the supplication of thy servant, and of thy people Israel.* <u>*When*</u>

[19]

*thy people Israel be smitten down before the enemy, because they have sinned against thee, and shall turn again to thee, and confess thy name, and pray, and make supplication unto thee in this house: Then hear thou in heaven, and forgive the sin of thy people Israel, and bring them **again** unto the land which thou gavest unto their fathers...*

*If they sin against thee, (for there is no man that sinneth not,) and thou be angry with them, and deliver them to the enemy, so that they carry them away captives unto the land of the enemy, **far or near**; Yet if they shall bethink themselves in the land whither they were carried captives, and repent, and make supplication unto thee in the land of them that carried them captives, saying, We have sinned, and have done perversely, we have committed wickedness. And so return unto thee with all their heart, and with all their soul, in the land of their enemies, which led them away captive, and pray unto thee toward their land, which thou gavest unto their fathers, the city which thou hast chosen, and the house which I have built for thy name. **Then** hear thou their prayer and their supplication in heaven thy dwelling place, and maintain their cause And forgive thy people that have sinned against thee,... and give them compassion before them who carried them captive, that they may have compassion on them. For they be thy people, and thine inheritance, which thou broughtest forth out of Egypt, from the midst of the furnace of iron: that thine eyes may be opened unto the supplication of thou servant, and unto the supplication of thou people Israel, to harken*

[20]

unto them in all that they call for unto them.
For thou didst separate them from among all
the people of the earth, to be thine inheritance,
as thou spakest by the hand of Moses thy
servant, when thou broughtest our fathers out
of Egypt, O LORD God. And it was so, that
when Solomon had made an end of praying all
this prayer and supplication unto the LORD, he
arose from before the altar of the LORD, from
kneeling on his knees with his hands spread up
to heaven. (1 Kings 8:23; 30, 32-34, 46-54;
emphasis added)

Israel was a united Kingdom, experiencing peace and prosperity during the time Solomon prayed his prayer. Yet it was at *this time* Solomon prayed and interceded on behalf of the Children of Israel as if he knew that one day they would forsake God and provoke Him to anger. An anger that would result in the Children of Israel being carried away captives unto the land of their enemy, *"far or near."* Note that Solomon also prays, *"**When** thy people Israel be smitten down before the enemy, because they have sinned against thee..."* as if Israel's disobedience was to be expected. He further prays that, if the children of Israel should *"bethink themselves"* and *"repent and return"* to the Lord with all their heart *"in the land whither they were carried captives,"* he asks God to **then** hear their prayer and *"maintain* [plead] *their cause."* That is, deliver, avenge, and do them justice (Gill, 1 Kings 8:45; emphasis added).

A third prophetic scripture that speaks to an end-time captivity for the Children of Israel is in Deuteronomy, Chapter 28. In this chapter, God

[21]

Himself forewarned the Children of Israel of captivity and of specific curses that would befall them if they failed to keep His commandments. He told them that **He** would bring a nation against them *from far, from the end of the earth, as swift as the eagle flieth; a nation whose tongue* they would not understand: "*A nation of fierce countenance, which shall not regard the person of the old, nor shew favour to the young*" (Duet. 28:49-50; emphasis added). He also forewarned the Children of Israel that **He** would "*scatter them from one end of the earth to the other,*" **via *ships*** where they would serve "*other gods which neither they nor their fathers had known*" (Deut. 28:64, 68; emphasis added).

Lastly, an apparent indication of an end-time captivity for the Children of Israel is found in Leviticus 26 Chapter verses 33, 38-45:

> *And I will scatter you among the heathen, and will draw out a sword after you: and your land shall be desolate, and your cities waste....And ye shall perish among the heathen and the land of your enemies shall eat you up. And they that are left of you shall pine away in their iniquity in your enemies' lands; and also in the iniquities of their fathers shall they pine away with them. If they shall confess their iniquity, and the iniquity of their fathers, with their trespass which they trespassed against me, and that also they have walked contrary unto me; And that I also have walked contrary unto them, and have brought them into the land of their enemies; if then their uncircumcised hearts be humbled, and they then accept of the*

[22]

punishment of their iniquity: Then will I remember my covenant with Jacob, and also my covenant with Isaac, and also my covenant with Abraham will I remember; and I will remember the land.

*The land also shall be left of them, and shall enjoy her sabbaths, while she lieth desolate without them: and they shall accept of the punishment of their iniquity: because, even because they despised my judgments, and because their soul abhorred my statutes .And yet for all that, when they be in the land of their enemies, I **will not** cast them away, **neither** will I abhor them, to destroy them utterly, and to break my covenant with them: for I am the LORD their God. But I will for their sakes remember the covenant of their ancestors, whom I brought forth out of the land of Egypt in the sight of the heathen, that I might be their God: I am the LORD.* (Emphasis added)

Today, the Children of Israel are in captivity or exile in the "*land of their enemies.*" Their present-day captivity historically began in AD 70 when the Roman army, led by General Caesar Titus, son of the Roman Emperor, Vespasian, seized the city of Jerusalem and burned down the second Temple. Flavius Josephus, the first-century Jewish historian, gives detailed accounts of the Jew-Roman Wars of 60-70 AD. He describes in ghastly detail how the Jewish state was brought to an end during this time (Whiston, 888-895). Further, it has been estimated that over 1,000,000 Jews fled into Africa to escape Roman persecution during the period from Pompey

[23]

to Julius (Windsor, 84). Over the course of time, Jews or Hebrew Israelites who fled into Africa eventually migrated and set up kingdoms primarily in West and South Africa. Historians and scholars alike have documented the presence of Hebrewism and **Hebrew Kingdoms** in West Africa. Below are a map showing an area known as **Negroland** in the **West Coast of Africa** in the **Guinea Slave Cost** and a 1747 map showing the **Kingdom of Judah** in the **West Africa** area known as "**Negroland.**"

Map: Negroland on the West Coast of Africa in Guinea Slave Coast

Figure 5: **Publication Author:** Bowen, Emanuel. List No. 3733.407 Series No. 50 Permission for use granted by David Rumsey Map Collection, www.davidrumsey.com.

1747 Map of the Kingdom of Juda (Judah) in West Africa in Guinea Slave Coast

Figure 6: **Publication Author:** Bowen, Emanuel. List No. 3733.407 Series No. 50 (modified). Used by Permission, David Ramsey Map Collection, www.davidrumsey.com. Also modified image address: arainasireach.files.wordpress.com/2014/04.

On the map, the **Kingdom of Juda** is seen located in the area named the **"Slave Coast."** A town named **Whidah** is also close to the coast. It was **a major slave-trading port** during the time of the transatlantic slave trade. Today the town is called **Ouidah**, which means Whydah or *Judah* ("Ouidah").

Some **Hebrew Kingdoms** in **West Africa** actually predate the era of Roman persecution. One such Kingdom is that of the **Bantu** people who migrated into Africa about the same time of the Exodus, having left Egypt prior to the enslavement of the Hebrews. When the Bantus came into Africa they controlled west, central, and south Africa. (Nasi). They ruled many of the great kingdoms of South Africa. Many of the inhabitants throughout Africa's west coast were eventually captured and taken as slaves to North America. Among the most numerous were the **Bantu** people. Over a wide-spread area of Southern states, Bantu placed names, which reflect the presence of their large numbers and indicate how the Bantus changed the landscape and culture of the white world that had enslaved them (*New World Encyclopedia*). Interestingly, Black South Africans were officially called "**Bantu**" by the Apartheid regime. However, new legislation and documents from the South African government have replaced "**Bantu**" with "Black" ("Bantu").

Other Hebrew Kingdoms in West Africa include the ancient **Black Jewish Empire of Ghana** that was established in the western Sudan. From about AD 300 on, it was ruled by a dynasty of Jewish Kings known as the Za Dynasty. The founder of the Dynasty was a man named Za el Yemeni, who descended from Jews of Yemen (Windsor, 87). Research by Dierk Lange, a professor of African History at the University of Bayreuth, Germany, has made it clear that the **Yoruba** of the Niger-Congo (Negroland) region had Semitic ancestors (579-595). The **Ashanti** tribe of West Africa also has Hebrew origins. For detailed descriptions of Ashanti Hebrew customs and many other tribes of West Africa, the reader is encouraged to read Joseph J. William's book, *Hebrewism of West Africa.*

The **Igbos** were yet another Hebrew presence in Africa. The Igbos were sometimes referred to as "Ibos, Ebos, Eboes, and Heebos" (Portal: Igbo). The latter is believed to be a corruption of the word

[26]

Hebrew (Alaezi, 54). In his book, *IBOS: Hebrew Exiles from Israel*, Alaezi mentions that the first British explorers who met the Ibos of Nigeria were quick to identify them... and so simply referred to them as Hebrews (Heebos, Eboes, and later Ibos) (54). Jewish sources also refer to the Igbos as Hebrews. For instance, the article "**Nigeria**" in the *Jewish Virtual Library*, which deals with *Igbo Jews*, reports, "According to oral traditions, the Ibo have resided in 'Iboland,' a region of modern-day Nigeria, for over 1500 years. Before that, the tradition asserts that they were migrants from ancient Israel" (Bard).

In a White House memo to President Nixon dated Tuesday, January 28, 1969, former Secretary of State, Henry Kissinger describes the *Igbo*s as "the wandering Jews of West Africa—gifted, aggressive, westernized, at best envied and resented, but mostly despised by their neighbours in the federation" ("Foreign Relations").

Owning to the effects of migration and the Atlantic slave trade, there are now ethnic Igbo populations in countries such as Cameroon and Equatorial Guinea as well as outside of Africa. Today, many African Americans and Afro Caribbeans are of Igbo descent ("Igbo People").

As we see, Hebrewism and Hebrew Kingdoms in West Africa have been documented by historians and scholars alike. Hebrews' migration into West Africa continued for nearly two thousand years following the AD 70 Roman persecution. Those desiring additional information on the topic of

Hebrew Kingdoms in West Africa, please refer to the Suggested Resource section of the book.

As been mentioned, an estimated one million Jews fled into Africa to escape Roman persecution, eventually migrating into West Africa. However, after settling in that land, many of the Hebrew Israelites did not retain their allegiance to God or His commandments. Some were influenced by the pagan and false religions of the native inhabitants. Some even introduced the wisdom and pagan religion they had learned from the Egyptians to colonies they established outside of Egypt. Others mixed pagan beliefs with the true religion of their Israelite ancestors (Nasi). There were those who also practiced the *offering up* of human sacrifices to the pagan god Moloch. Because of their continual disobedience and idolatry, God allowed the covenant curses in Deuteronomy (28) and Leviticus (26) to befall them just as He forewarned, if they did not keep his laws, statutes, and commandments *wherever* they went. The covenant curses are still being experienced by the Children of Israel, and the curses clearly identify who and where they are today. While the descendants of Jacob are presently experiencing **_all_** the curses of Deuteronomy and Leviticus, we will call to the reader's attention just a few from Deuteronomy 28, which should leave no doubt in anyone's mind who the *scriptures* point to as being the Children of Israel and thus the true Jews today. God said that these curses would be *"for a sign and a wonder"* [i.e., an identifier] upon the Children of Israel and their seed *forever* (Deut. 28:46).

Note the following (uncanny) commentary by John Gill—an English Baptist pastor, theologian and bible scholar of the *1700s*—regarding this particular verse:

> ...those CURSES before pronounced, and what follow, should rest and REMAIN upon them, CONTINUE with them, and be VERY VISIBLE on them; so as to be OBSERVED by others, as a SIGN of the wrath and displeasure of God, and of the FULFILMENT of prophecy, and of the TRUTH of divine revelation: and so "for a wonder" as it is most astonishing to observe how EXACTLY all the curses threatened them have FALLEN upon them and have ABODE with them, as they did in their FORMER captivities, and more ESPECIALLY do in the PRESENT one and, what is the greater wonder, that notwithstanding these dreadful calamities and SO-LONG CONTINUED, enough to have crushed any people from being a people yet they have CONTINUED, and STILL do continue, a distinct people; which is a STANDING miracle, and one would think SUFFICIENT to convince the most hardened and obstinate deist of the TRUTH and authority of the sacred Scriptures; in which stand so many GLARING PROPHESIES that have been FULFILED, and are CONTINUALLY FULFILLING in this people. (Emphasis added)

Some of the curses in Deuteronomy 28 are highlighted below, after a review of the conditions under which God said He would bring a blessing or a curse upon the Children of Israel:

[29]

Deut. 28:1-2: *Condition for Blessings: And it shall come to pass, if thou shalt hearken diligently unto the voice of the Lord thy God, to observe and to do all his commandments which I command thee this day, that the Lord thy God will set thee on high above all nations of the earth: And all these blessings shall come on thee, and overtake thee, if thou shalt hearken unto the voice of the Lord thy God.*

Duet. 28:15: *Condition for Curses: But it shall come to pass, if thou wilt not hearken unto the voice of the LORD thy God, to observe to do all his commandments and his statutes which I command thee this day; that all these curses shall come upon thee, and overtake thee:* (Emphasis added)

Thus, obedience to God's Commandments, statutes, and laws was the condition for the Children of Israel's blessings. Disobedience was the condition for the covenant curses.

Now, we shall highlight some of the specific curses that have befallen upon the Children of Israel because of their disobedience to God. Remember, scripture says these curses will be a "SIGN" (an identifier), and a wonder upon these people and their seed *"FOREVER."*

Specific Curses of Deuteronomy 28

Duet. 28:25-26: *The LORD shall cause thee to be smitten before thine enemies: thou shalt go out one way against them, and flee seven ways before them: and shalt be removed into all the kingdoms of the earth. And thy carcass shall be*

[30]

meat unto all fowls of the air, and unto the
beasts of the earth, and no man shall fray them
away. (Emphasis added)

Here the Lord is saying that the Children of
Israel shall be *defeated* before their enemies. They
will go out one way against their enemies but will
flee several ways before them. Thus, *they will win*
no battles (or lasting battles) and shall *be removed*
or scattered *into all the kingdoms* (nations) *of the*
earth. Moreover, their carcasses will be food to all
the birds in the sky and to the beasts of the Earth,
which no one will be able to frighten away. This
reminds me of the thousands of lynchings done to
Black men and women down through the years,
some merely for sport. Their dead and sometimes
charred and mutilated bodies were left hanging
from trees to be food for all of the birds and beasts
of the Earth, with no one to *"fray them away."* The
song "Strange Fruit" captures the essence of this
horror.

> Deut. 28:29-30: *And thou shalt grope at*
> *noonday, as the blind gropeth in darkness, and*
> *thou shalt not prosper in thy ways: and thou*
> *shalt be only oppressed and spoiled evermore,*
> *and no man shall save thee. Thou shalt betroth*
> *a wife, and another man shall lie with her:*
> *thou shalt build a house, and thou shalt not*
> *dwell therein: thou shalt plant a vineyard, and*
> *shalt not gather the grapes thereof.* (Emphasis
> added)

Here the Lord is saying that the Children of
Israel will grope at noon, as the blind man gropes in
darkness—they will have difficulty finding their

way. They will not prosper in their ways but will only be oppressed and robbed continually. I'm reminded that, although a few "African Americans" may make it to the top, when they come to the end of their life, they are typically left penniless and/or in great debt (e.g., James Brown, Redd Fox, Michael Jackson, Sammy Davis, Jr.). And, what other race of people has known oppression like "African Americans"—from slavery to Jim Crow, from racial discrimination to "the illusion of inclusion" to systematic and institutionalized discrimination?—*and none* will save or deliver them from their predicament. Finally, the Israelite man shall marry a wife but *another* man will violate her. The Children of Israel shall build a house, but will not live in it; will plant a vineyard, but will not use its fruit. *Did not all of these things happen to the "Negro" in the days of slavery?*

> Deut. 28:32: *Thy sons and thy daughters shall be given unto another people, and thine eyes shall look, and fail with longing for them all the day long; and there shall be no might in thine hand.*

This also happened in the days of slavery when the enslaved "Negroes" had to stand helplessly by and watch their sons and daughters be sold off to another owner.

> Deut. 28:37: *And thou shalt become an astonishment, a proverb, and a byword among all nations whither the LORD shall lead thee.*

Here the Lord is telling the Children of Israel that they will become an object of horror, scorn, and ridicule among all the peoples where HE, *the LORD*, will drive them. "Blacks," when brought over as slaves, were likened unto "savages," "monkeys," and "apes," and many were fearful of them. And what other race of people has had to endure so much ridicule and be subjected to insulting epithets or name-calling such as "darkies," the N word, "coon," "sambo," "ape/monkey," etc., and to name changes (Negro, Colored, Black, Afro American, African American) as the once-called "Negroes"? — Thus, becoming "*a byword.*"

> Deut. 28:41: *Thou shalt beget sons and daughters, but thou shalt not enjoy them; for they shall go into captivity.*

Here the Lord is saying to the Children of Israel that they will father children who will not remain with them so they can enjoy them because they will be taken into captivity as *slaves or as prisoners*. This again was evidenced during the time of slavery, when children of Blacks were taken from them and sold away. Now, today, many Black parents watch their children taken captive into the prison system, oftentimes for petty or no real crimes. Also, far too many Black youth and young men today go into the captivity of a premature grave at the hands of slaying cops.

> Deut. 28:43-44: <u>*The stranger that is within thee shall get up above thee very high; and thou shalt come down very low*</u>*. He shall lend to thee, and thou shalt not lend to him:* <u>*he shall be the head, and thou shalt be the tail.*</u>
> (Emphasis added)

[33]

Here the Lord is saying to the Children of Israel that the *foreigner* who resides among them will rise higher and higher above them while they sink lower and lower in social and economic status. We see such a phenomenon today, when foreigners who come to America quickly establish and own businesses primarily in Black communities, while Black-owned businesses are hardly anywhere to be found. Foreigners are represented in the United State government and the U.S. Supreme Court, where Black representation is sparse to nonexistent. Blacks rank the highest in unemployment and in poverty and are usually the lowest on the totem pole in the workplace in terms of salary and job positions. He, *the foreigner, shall lend to them*, and the Children of Israel will not be in any economic or financial position to lend to them. *The foreigner shall also be the head and the Children of Israel shall be the tail*. Blacks represent the poorest in the land and the lowest in terms of economic and employment status; fewer of them are hired for or promoted to professional or corporate positions; fewer of them own businesses or are prominent in health care, and so on. As a people, Blacks are not the head but the tail, no matter where they are or in what country they live.

> Deut. 28:45-46: *Moreover, <u>all these curses shall come upon thee</u>, and <u>shall pursue thee</u>, and <u>overtake thee</u>, till thou be destroyed; because thou hearkenedst not unto the voice of the LORD thy God, to keep his commandments and his statutes which he commanded thee: And they shall be upon thee <u>for a sign and for a wonder, and upon thy seed for ever</u>.*

[34]

Please refer to John Gill's commentary on page 29, regarding this verse.

> Deut. 28:48: *Therefore <u>shalt thou serve thine enemies</u> which <u>the</u> LORD <u>shall send against thee</u>, in hunger, and in thirst, and in nakedness, and in want of all things: <u>and he shall put a yoke of iron upon thy neck</u>, until he have destroyed thee.* (Emphasis added)

The Lord is saying to the Children of Israel that they will serve their enemies whom *He will send* against them (not only the Assyrians, Chaldean/Babylonians, and the Romans of the past but also their latter-day enemies as well). This is inclusive of all the Gentile nations and their descendants that were, *and who still are*, part of the enslavement of His People—enemies, which were identified in Psalm 83:1-8. Because of their disobedience, the Children of Israel *shall serve their enemies* whom the LORD will send against them, *in hunger, in thirst, in nakedness, and in the lack of all things*. Furthermore, He (*the Lord God*), will put an iron yoke on their neck until *He* has destroyed them. (See Jer. 28:10-14). In other words, the Lord will cause the *enemies* of the Children of Israel to put a yoke of iron around their necks. This could mean both a literal yoke of iron such as was seen in the days of slavery and a yoke of subjugation to their enemies, which would be just as intolerable, and from which they would not be able to free themselves—as is seen by their present-day captivity (Gill, Deut. **28:48**).

> Deut. 28:49: *The LORD shall bring a nation against thee from far, from the end of the*

[35]

earth, as swift as the eagle flieth; a nation whose tongue thou shalt not understand;

Here the Lord is saying to the Children of Israel that **He** will bring a nation against *them from afar, from the end of the earth.* This would seem to preclude any of the surrounding nations of their day. This nation shall come *from afar* and *as swift as the eagle flieth.* Just as an eagle hastens to its prey, this nation will hasten upon the Children of Israel as to a prey, to devour and destroy her as a nation or as a people. It is a nation *whose tongue or language* that they shall not understand (Gill, Deut. 28:49). This curse saw some fulfillment during the days of the Bible as well as during more recent modern-day history. Thus, the force and drive with which the Chaldeans seized upon and the Romans destroyed Jerusalem are like the force and drive with which the confederation of nations seized upon the coast of Africa, capturing and enslaving Hebrew Israelites. Whereas the eagle was the insignia of the Roman army, the eagle is also the insignia of America, who participated in preying on the enslaved Hebrew Israelites.

Deut. 28:50: *A nation of fierce countenance, which shall not regard the person of the old, nor shew favour to the young...*

Here the Lord God is telling the Children of Israel that He will bring a *ruthless nation* of fierce countenance against them. This can be said of the Chaldeans, who were a nation *dreadful and terrible,* (Hab. 1:7). This can be said of the Roman empire— the fourth beast, as noted in Daniel 7:7, who was a terror to all the world: (Gill, Deut. 28:50). This can also be said of America and other nations who showed no respect for Blacks, old or young, during the days of slavery and who show no respect even now. The founder of the Lest We Forget Black Holocaust Slavery Museum in Philadelphia PA., vividly documents how the slave master would steal babies of slaves and actually use them as bait to catch alligators for their skins (Ragsdale). Suggested resources for further research on the topic include "Alligator Bait," *Jim Crow Museum of Racist Memorabilia* Ferris State University and "Black Babies Used as Alligator Bait in Florida" by Chuck Strouse, *Miami New Times*. Thus, just as the slave masters whipped the backs of males and females, old and young alike, today Blacks—young Black males in particular—are disproportionately suspended from school, incarcerated, brutalized, and slain at a frequent and alarming rate by police officers who show no respect for the young or the old.

> *Verse 64: And the LORD shall scatter thee among all people, from the one end of the earth even unto the other; and there thou shalt serve other gods, which neither thou nor thy fathers have known, even wood and stone.*

Here the Lord God is telling the Children of Israel that **HE** will scatter them among all peoples *from one end of the earth even unto the other*. This refers to the Children of Israel's present-day dispersion, having now been scattered to the four corners of the Earth—east, west, north, and south. There they would worship other gods of wood and stone, which neither they nor their fathers knew,

[37]

such as the idols of the Papists, their images of the Virgin Mary and departed saints, made of wood and stone, and the consecrated wafer which their forefathers never knew (Gill, Duet. 28:64). "Other gods," unknown to their forefathers, would include other religions, such as Mormonism, New Age, Islam, and many of the Protestant religions.

> *Verse 65: And among these nations shalt thou find no ease, neither shall the sole of thy foot have rest: but the LORD shall give thee there a trembling heart, and failing of eyes, and sorrow of mind...*

Here the Lord God is telling the Children of Israel that they would find no peace among the nations where He would bring them. In those nations, *He* would give them a trembling or fearful heart. They would live in constant fear of persecution, oppression, harassment, and so on. They would have failing eyes—looking in vain for someone who would champion their cause and deliver them from all their fears and troubles. They would have sorrow of mind because of their captivity, afflictions, oppression, and injustices.

Deviating just for a moment from the curses in Deuteronomy, below are verses highlighted from Isaiah and Zechariah, which also contain curses pertaining to the Children of Israel and their present-day captivity.

> *Isaiah 42:22 But this is a people robbed and spoiled; they are all of them snared in holes, and <u>they are hid in prison houses: they are for a prey, and none delivers</u>; for a spoil, <u>and none says, "Restore.</u>"* (Emphasis added)

[38]

The Children of Israel have been kidnapped and robbed of their possession, treasures, identity, and heritage (for now). *"They are hid in prison houses"* speaks again to massive over-incarceration of Blacks in prisons throughout the nation. According to a U.S. Census, African-American men comprise a mere 6% of the American population but make up nearly half of the 2 million inmates in U.S. jails or prisons. Also, according to the U.S., the ratio for young Black male imprisonment is around 10 percent or 10,000 prisoners per 100,000. Blacks are about 12-13% of the general population but make up *72%* of a combined jail (35%) and prison (37%) inmate population ("Statistics"). A greater percentage of Blacks are also in for-profit or private prisons, where the corporation grosses a per-year fee for each inmate. Thus, they are a spoil and a prey for all the nations to exploit for their own profit, a commodity to be used for inhumane government-backed and/or -controlled experiments, such as the Tuskegee Syphilis Experiment, irradiation, and other "research" that is particularly carried out upon Black prison inmates. And none say *deliver*, none say *RESTORE*, give back, return, or amend.

> *Whose possessors slay them, and hold themselves not guilty and they that sell them say, Blessed be the LORD; for I am rich: and their **own** shepherds pity them not.* (Zech. 11:5; emphasis added)

Here the Lord God is saying to the Children of Israel that those who buy, slaughter, or kill them are not punished and do not hold themselves guilty of their murderous crimes. Those who sell them say, *"Praise the LORD because I have become rich!"* Even their own shepherds (i.e. Spiritual/Religious and/or Political leaders) have no compassion for them. Consider the time when lynching Blacks was nothing more than a sport or a form of entertainment by their slayers. Today, cops have the "luxury" of slaying and criminally abusing Blacks with NO fear of facing any criminal charges or being convicted of any crime, while their slain victims are blamed for the criminal acts done against them. Thus, their "possessors" slay them and hold THEMSELVES not guilty.

> *Deut. 28 Verse 68: And the LORD shall bring thee into Egypt again with ships, by the way whereof I spake unto thee, Thou shalt see it no more again: and there ye shall be sold unto your enemies for bondmen and bondwomen, and no man shall buy you.* (Emphasis added)

Egypt is referred to as *"the house of bondage"* ten times in scripture (Exodus 13:3, 14; Exodus 20:2; Deuteronomy 5:6; Deuteronomy 6:12; Deuteronomy 8:14; Deuteronomy 13: 5, 10; Joshua 24:17 and Judges 6:8). Thus, the word, "Egypt" used in Deuteronomy 28:68 is not referring to a country but to a condition—a condition of bondage. Here the Lord God is saying to the Children of Israel that **HE** will bring them into Egypt—*"the house of bondage"* again, *WITH SHIPS* (i.e. slave ships) by a route or a way that they *would not see again*. Here, "The Door of No Return" on Goree Island comes to mind. Once captured, Israelites entered the "Door" and would not return or see their home again.

Rather they would be taken to a land where they would be sold to *"their enemies."*

I suspect that *the enemies* of the Children of Israel in these present days are none other than the *descendants of their enemies* named in the Bible (i.e., Edom, Moab, Ishmael, Ammon, Tyre, Sidon, and Philista). Scripture said that the Children of Israel *will be sold* **to their enemies** as *bondmen and bondwomen* (i.e., slaves) and *"**No Man Shall Buy You**"*. This phrase refers to the Levitical Law of Redemption found in Leviticus Chapter 25. According to the law, if an Israelite was forced to sell part of his property or forced to sell himself into slavery, his nearest of kin could intercede or step in and "buy back" what he was forced to sell. Thus, if an Israelite was forced into slavery, his redeemer (next of kin) purchased his freedom. However, for the Children of Israel, God says *no man shall buy them.* That is, no man shall deliver, save, or lift them out of their present captivity. Though some men (Abraham Lincoln, Marcus Garvey, Malcom X, Martin Luther King, Jr., and President Kennedy) have tried, they were not completely successful. We shall see later, however, that Israel's deliverance from her present-day captivity will come by the very Hand of the Most High Himself.

God himself forewarned the Children of Israel that *He* would scatter them to the four corners of the Earth and *all* the curses in Deuteronomy Chapter 28 would fall upon them *and their seed forever* if they failed to keep His statutes, laws, and commandments. Moreover, all these curses would follow them *wherever* they went *as a sign* to the other nations. The Jews/Hebrew Israelites who fled into Africa following the Roman persecution of AD 70 and eventually migrated into west, central, and south Africa, for the most part did not retain their allegiance to God over the years. Therefore, God allowed all the curses of Deuteronomy 28 (and Leviticus 26) to befall them *and their seed*. Thus, as foretold in Deuteronomy, their descendants today continue to experience the covenant curses in *the lands of their enemies*. The Children of Israel or the Hebrew Israelites are none other than Blacks who fell victim to the transatlantic (and the Indian Ocean) slave trade—Hebrew Israelites who were *scattered* throughout the nations of the world *via ships* and sold as *bondmen and bondwomen*, just as God forewarned. They are now known as African Americans, Haitians, Jamaicans, and Dominicans, just to name a few. Thus, God used the transatlantic and Indian Ocean slave trade as the vehicle to scatter His Chosen people to the four corners of the Earth, just as He said he would because of their disobedience to Him (see map).

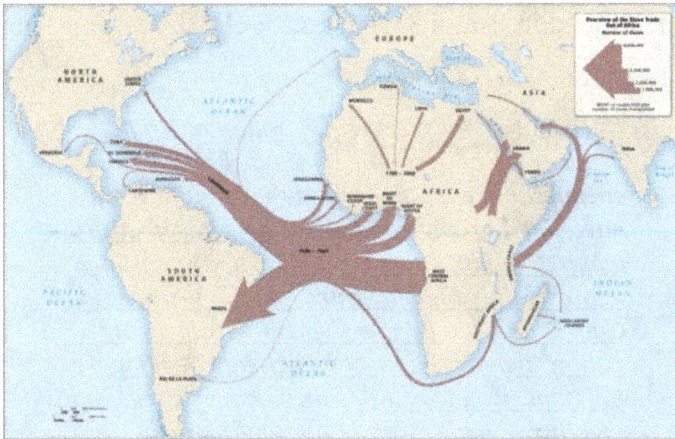

Figure 7: Eltis and Richardson, Atlas of the Transatlantic Slave Trade (2010), Map 1. Yale University Press. Used with permission. All rights reserved.

The slave trade helped fulfill a covenant curse upon the Children of Israel forewarned by God some 3,000 years earlier: *"And **the Lord** shall scatter thee… from one end of the earth even unto the other"*(Deut.28:64). As mentioned, His Providential Hand is in everything that takes place in the world. *No worldly* event happens by chance. Given this, can you imagine that a massive removal of basically an entire nation of people taken as captives from one land and sold as slaves (i.e., bondmen and bondwomen) to other nations would not be an event significant enough to have been foretold in the Bible or ordained by God? Such, in fact, is the case. The Transatlantic (and Indian Ocean) slave trade is duly noted in scripture and justifiably ordained by God (Isa. 42:24-25). Besides

[43]

the verses of scripture just reviewed from Deuteronomy 28:15-68, the slave trade is also mentioned in Psalm 83:1-8 and Joel 3:3-7.

Psalms 83:1-8 reads:

> *Keep not thou silence, O God: hold not thy peace, and be not still, O God. For, lo, thine enemies make a tumult: and they that hate thee have lifted up thy head. They have taken crafty counsel against thy people, and consulted against thy **hidden ones**. They have said, Come, and let us cut them off from being a nation; that the name of Israel may be no more in remembrance. For they have consulted together with one consent: they are confederate against thee: The tabernacles of Edom, and the Ishmaelites; of Moab, and the Hagarenes; Gebal, and Ammon, and Amalek; the Philistines with the inhabitants of Tyre; Assur also is joined with them: they have holpen the children of Lot. Selah.* (Emphasis added)

The above scripture speaks of a confederation of nations that took crafty council against God's people and consulted against his "hidden ones." His "hidden ones" denote the Children of Israel—God's Chosen People. This confederation of nations named above said, *"Come let us cut them off from being a nation that the name of Israel may no more be in remembrance."* In other words, their sole purpose for coming together was to devise a plan to annihilate Israel from the face of the Earth, *to be remembered* no more. This seems to have been (and continues to be) a desire and a goal of the enemies of the Children of Israel since their beginning. After

[44]

all, it is the nation and a people from which the Messiah, the Savior of World would and did come in the flesh.

An inscription by the ancient Egyptian king Merneptah who reigned from 1213 to 1203 BC was found on the Merneptah Stele (also known as the Israel Stele or Victory Stele of Merneptah). Line 27 of its inscription reads, "Israel is laid waste and his seed is not" ("Merneptah Stele"). Though some may debate exactly who or what is being referred to in the inscription, it does seem to convey a desire held by the enemies of Israel down through the ages to this present time: *"Come let us cut them off from being a nation that the name (or the people) of Israel will be no more in remembrance."* This **is** a timeless goal and desire of Israel's enemies and continues to be actively and aggressively pursued to this very day. The annihilation of a people by whatever means necessary is the ultimate goal.

The above verse may also make some allusion to the physical and psychological genocidal attempts that have been purposely perpetrated against Blacks or the once-called Negroes throughout history. Such physical and mental genocidal attempts have come via whitewashing and the misrepresentation of Black history and Blacks' accomplishments and the constant portrayal of Blacks in a negative light in the media, Jim Crow and lynchings. Police slayings of Black men and children as young as 12, the mass and over-incarceration of Blacks in the criminal-justice system, forced vaccinations of questionable content, and abortion industries targeting Black

[45]

neighborhoods, where an estimated *16 million or more* abortions have been performed on Black women since 1973 (Childress) are still other genocidal attempts.

Psalm 83:5 continues to say, *"For they have consulted together with ONE CONSENT; they are confederate against thee."* The Psalmist in the scriptures makes it clear that, though the confederation's aim was against Israel (to cut it off from being a nation); it was seen as a confederation against the Most High Himself. Note also that the nations comprising the confederation were *"the enemies"* of Israel. Thus, again, is it not conceivable that the nations, who *"consulted together with one consent"* regarding the Slave Trade and then sold the seed or the descendants of Jacob into slavery were the descendants of Israel's enemies named in Psalm 83? Scripture did say that the Children of Israel would be sold to *"their enemies"* as bondmen and bondwomen (Deut. 28:68). Therefore, it is conceivable that *both* the slave traders and the slave masters were merely the physical descendants of Israel's enemies named in the Bible. This suggests that current or modern-day history is a continuation or a reflection of Bible history. Scripture tells us that there is *nothing* new under the sun. *The thing that hath been, it is that which shall be; and that which is done is that which shall be done: and there is no new thing under the sun* (Eccles. 1:9).

Joel 3:1-7 reads:

> *For, behold, in those days, and in that time, when I shall bring again the captivity of Judah*

[46]

and Jerusalem, I will also gather all nations,
and will bring them down into the valley of
Jehoshaphat, and will plead with them there
for my people and for my heritage Israel,
whom they have scattered among the nations,
and parted my land And they have cast lots for
my people; and have given a boy for an harlot,
and sold a girl for wine, that they might drink.
*Yea, and what have ye to do with me, **O Tyre,***
and Zidon, and all the coasts of Palestine?
***will ye render me a recompence?** and if ye*
recompense me, swiftly and speedily will I
return your recompence upon your own head.
Because ye have taken my silver and my gold,
and have carried into your temples my goodly
pleasant things. The children also of Judah
and the children of Jerusalem have ye sold
*unto the Grecians, **that ye might remove them***
***far from their border.** Behold, I will raise*
them out of the place whither ye have sold
them, and will return your recompence upon
your own head: (Emphasis added)

Some believe that the aforementioned scriptures found in Psalms 83 and Joel 3 have already been fulfilled. However, it is important to keep in mind that sometimes with respect to Bible prophecy the same prophecy can have a more immediate fulfillment in the day that it was prophesied as well as a latter day or end-time fulfillment. Such is the case with the prophecy regarding the destruction of Tyrus/Tyre in Ezekiel 26:1-21. This being said below is a commentary by William MacDonald concerning Joel 3:1-7.

God will gather the Gentile Nations to the Valley of Jehoshaphat and will judge them for

[47]

their treatment of the Jews. Tyre, Sidon, and Philistia will be recompensed for *plundering and enslaving God's people.* The people in those cities, would in turn, be sold as slaves—a fitting punishment for their crime. (1110; emphasis added)

At this point it becomes necessary to digress and review the genealogy of Noah's three sons in order to disclose or uncover those who were involved in the transatlantic slave trade and their respective roles. Genesis 9:18-19 says, *"And the sons of Noah that went forth of the ark were **Shem**, and **Ham**, and **Japheth:** and Ham is the father of Canaan. These are the three sons of Noah: and of them was the whole earth overspread"* (emphasis added).

Let us begin with Noah's son Japheth, who is the progenitor of the Indo-Europeans. The chart below shows Japheth's descendants. The chart also shows that the **Ashkenazi "Jews"** are descendants of Noah's son **Japheth** through his son Gomer. Remember, too, scripture refers to Japheth and his descendants as Gentiles (Gen. 10: 2-5).

[48]

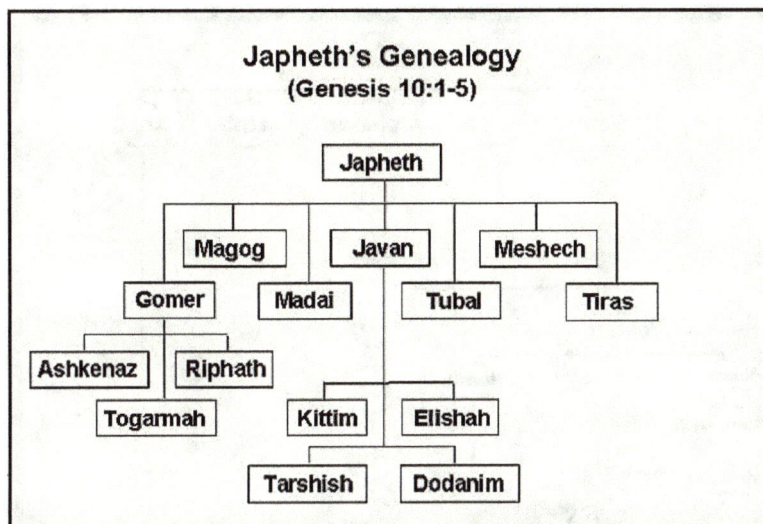

Figure 8: Chart from the Genesis 1-11 course by Bill Mandakis, http://www.bjm-home.com/genesis/genesistoc.html. (Color added). Used by permission (granted 4/21/16).

Genealogy of Shem
(Gen. 10:21-31, 11:10-32; 1 Chr.1:17-28, 34, 2:1)

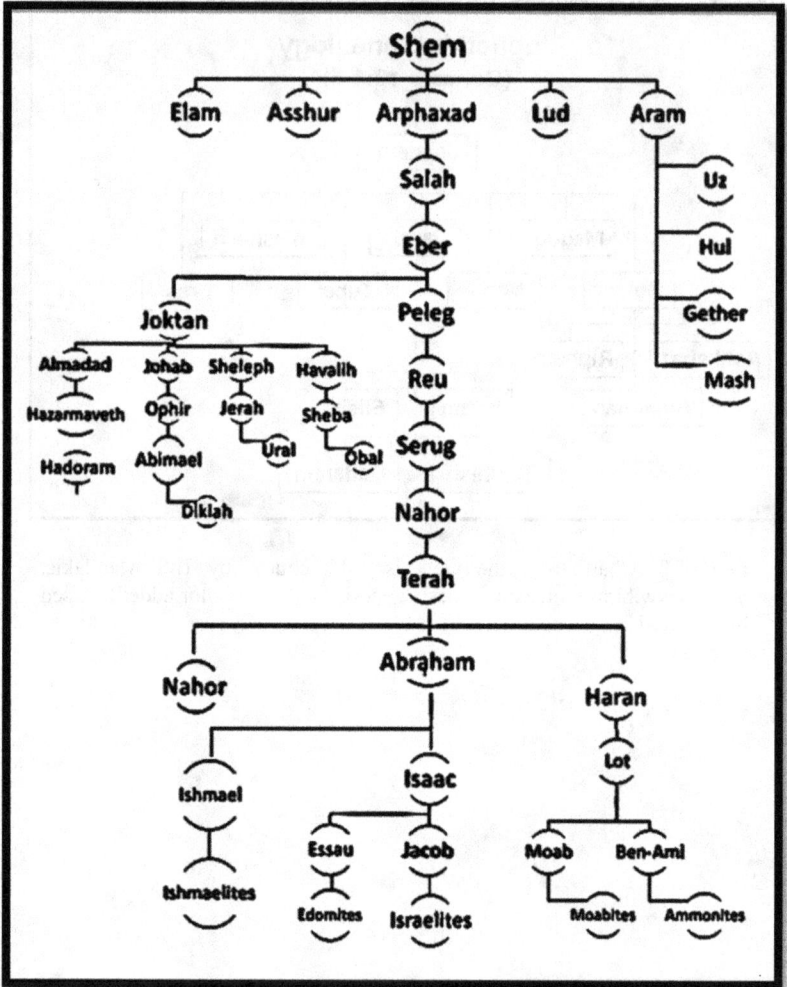

Figure 9: Genealogy of Shem chart designed by Myra Dillingham, Jan 11, 2017.

Shem is the progenitor of the Semitic race, which means that all descendants of Shem are Semitic. This includes the Elamites (Elam), the Ishmaelites (Ishmael), the Edomites (Esau/Edom), the Moabites (Moab), Ammonites (Ammon) and the Israelites (Jacob), to name a few (see chart).

Although *all* descendants of Shem are Semitic, *not all* descendants of Shem are Hebrews, Hebrew Israelites, or "Jews." Eber, Shem's great grandson, who is also called Heber in Luke 3:35, is the eponymous ancestor or Father of all the Hebrews (Larue). Abraham, however, was the first to be called a Hebrew in the Bible (Gen. 14:13). All the descendants of Eber would be considered Hebrews. Thus, the Ishmaelites, the Edomites, the Moabites, the Ammonites, and the Israelites were all Hebrews. Note however, that *only* Jacob and the descendants of *Jacob* were *Israelites* or Hebrew Israelites (see chart). The Israelites or Hebrew Israelites were also known as the Children of Israel or God's chosen people. The term "Jew," initially, was used only in reference to the tribe of Judah but later became a descriptor for all twelve tribes of Israel. Thus, the *Israelites* or *Hebrew Israelites are* the descendants of *Jacob's* twelve sons and again are also known as the Children of Israel, the Nation of Israel, the House of Jacob, the Jews, or God's Chosen People. We now turn our attention to the genealogy of Noah's son Ham.

According to two Bible dictionaries quoted below, **Ham** is the progenitor of the African or dark races of people but **NOT** the **NEGRO**.

Zondervan Compact Bible Dictionary defines Ham as

> The youngest son of Noah, born probably about 96 years before the Flood; and one of eight persons to live through the Flood. He became the progenitor of the dark races; *not the Negroes*, but the *Egyptians, Ethiopians, Libyans and Canaanites.* (213; emphasis added) [Used by permission of Zondervan.com. All rights reserved].

Young's Bible Dictionary defines Ham as

> A son of Noah and father of Cush, Egypt, Put, and Canaan. While they may have all been dark skinned, *they were not the forefather of the Negroid race*, but rather of peoples associated with Egypt in the N [*sic*] of the continent of Africa. (255-256; emphasis added) [Used by permission of Tyndale House Publishers, Inc. All rights reserved].

On the following page is a Genealogy chart of Ham's descendants. **Ham** is the progenitor of the Egyptians (Mizraim), **Libyans** (Put), Ethiopians (Cush) and the Canaanites (Canaan). Please note that the Libyans, the descendants of Put and the two named sons of Mizraim/Egypt (**Ludim, Lehabim**) were all a **Hamitc** people and not separate or distinct from Ham as some "scholars" try to imply. While all of Ham's sons—(**Mizraim/Egypt**, **Put**, Cush and Canaan) may have been dark skinned or black, they **were not** the forefathers of the Negroid race **nor** was Ham the progenitor of the Negroes according to scripture **and** the scholarly definitions of Ham above.

[52]

Genealogy Chart of Ham's Descendants

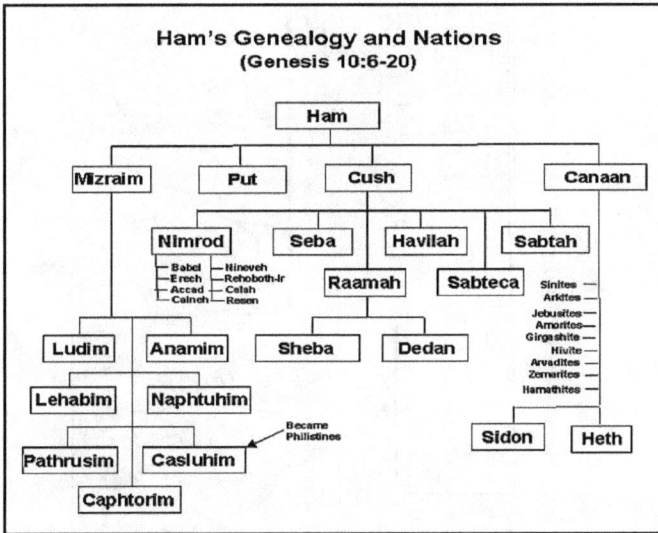

Figure 10: Chart from the Genesis 1-11 Course by Bill Mandakis, http://www.bjm-home.com/genesis/genesistoc.html. Color added. Used with permission (granted 4/21/16).

Therefore, the so-called "Negroes" *are not* descendants of Noah's son Ham as they were led to believe. Thus, they *are not Africans* or descendants of the Ancient Egyptians, as these were a *Hamitic* people (Gen10:6-20). The "Negro" also is *not* a descendant of Japheth, who is the progenitor of the Indo-Europeans (Gen. 10:2-5). Therefore that leaves only one son—**Shem** (Gen 9:18-19). Below is another image depicting Hebrew Israelite slaves in Egypt. Note that it is the *same* image shown earlier in the book on page 13, not colorized.

Semitic Race Making and Carrying Bricks

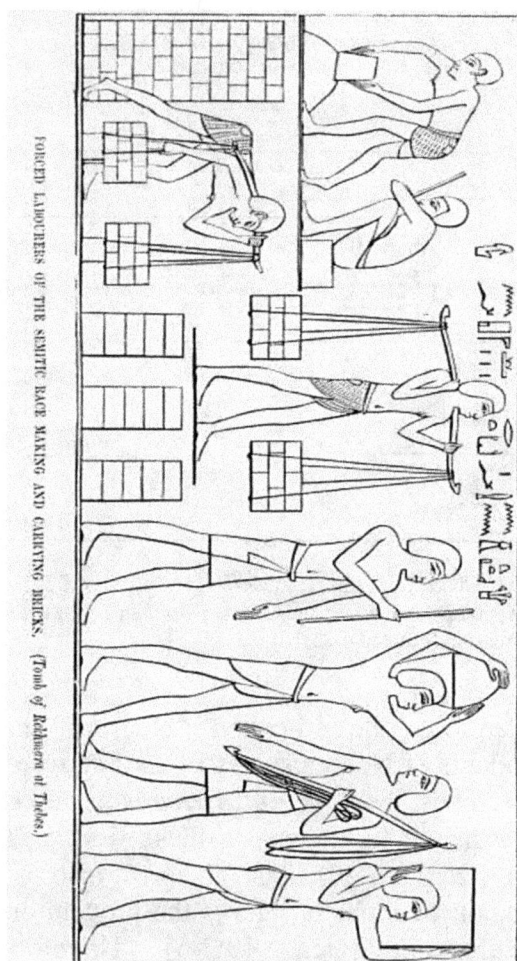

Figure 11: Ebers, Georg. Egypt: Descriptive, Historical, and Picturesque, Volume 1 Cassel & Company Limited New York. File: "Forced Labourers of the Semitic race stamping out Bricks" (1878)-, p 104, Travelers in the Middle East Archive (TIMEA). <http://hdl.handle.net/1911/21131>, Accessed April 28, 2015. This work is licensed under a CC-BY-- 2.5 license.

Look closely at the caption inside the picture itself. It reads "FORCED LABOURERS OF THE *SEMITIC* RACE MAKING AND CARRYING BRICKS. (Tomb of Rekhmire of Thebes)" [bold emphasis added]. Also, look at the second half of the picture, printed on page 56. The original source for this image is volume I of an 1878 work, entitled *Egypt: Descriptive, Historical, and Picturesque*, by Georg Ebers (104). The caption **inside** this picture reads, FORCED LABOURERS OF THE *SEMITIC* RACE STAMPING OUT BRICKS (Tomb of Rekhmire of Thebes)."

These pictures provide more evidence that the "Negro" is a Semitic race of people. That is, they are descendants of Shem and NOT Ham. They also confirm the fact that the Semitic people enslaved by the Ancient Egyptians were a black race of people as were the Ancient Egyptians.

Figure 12: Ebers, Georg. Egypt: Descriptive, Historical, and Picturesque, Volume 1 Cassel & Company Limited New York. File: "Forced Labourers of the Semitic race stamping out Bricks" (1878), p. 104, Travelers in the Middle East Archive (TIMEA). <http://hdl.handle.net/1911/21132>, Accessed April 28, 2015. This work is licensed under a CC-BY- 2.5 license.

As mentioned earlier, about one million Jews or Hebrew Israelites fled into Africa to escape Roman persecution. They eventually migrated and established kingdoms in Western and South Africa over the course of time. Later, they fell victim to the slave trade and were scattered throughout the four corners of the Earth and sold as bondmen and bondwomen. *Thus, Africans were not selling other Africans into slavery.* Africans (the descendants of Ham) were *knowingly* selling Hebrew Israelites (the descendants and seed of Jacob) into slavery, fulfilling the curse of Deuteronomy 28 that God said would befall them for their idolatry and disobedience to His statues and laws Thus, they were *sold to their enemies,* as *bondmen and bondwomen*—brought into *"Egypt,"* the house of bondage, AGAIN, via **Ships**.

Therefore, with respect to the slave trade, the Hebrew Israelites, while dispersed in Africa, were first enslaved by *Hamitic* Africans, who sold them to the *Arabs* [descendants of Ishmael]. The Arabs served as intermediaries between the Hamitic enslavers and *the European American [Grecian]* buyers [descendants of Japheth] ("Images"). It has been asserted by some that the *European "Jews"* (descendants of Japheth) totally dominated the trade in slaves to America. They were said to have been the major sellers and owners of slaves as well as merchant owners and operators of slave ships. To research the topic, the following are suggested: *African Presence in Early Europe* by Ivan Van Sertima, *Journal of African Civilizations,* Nov. 1985, Vol. 7, No. 2; *Documents Illustrative of the*

[57]

History of the Slave Trade to America by Elizabeth Donnan; *The Secret Relationship Between Blacks and Jews* by the Historical Research Department of NOI.

As was mentioned, a great majority of slaves were Bantus. The Igbo in the Atlantic slave trade also became one of the main groups enslaved in the era lasting between the 16th and late 19th century. They were dispersed to colonies such as Jamaica, Cuba, Hispaniola, Barbados, the United States, Belize, Trinidad, and Tobago, among others. In the United States, the Igbo were commonly found in the states of Maryland and Virginia ("Igbo people"). In the 1700s, out of 37,000 enslaved Blacks who arrived in Virginia from Calabar (in what is now Nigeria), 30,000 were Igbo. Virginia also had slaves from the *Yoruba*, the *Akan* area, Mande, Fulani, *Angola*, the Congo basin, and Madagascar (Chambers, 23).

A review of the Trans-Atlantic Slave Trade Database shows that the place of origin for slaves was hardly ever identified. However whenever the place of origin *was* identified, it shows the slaves to be mainly of "Eboo or Hebo" origin (*Trans-Atlantic 2013*). Additionally, it was not uncommon for the ancient Hebrew Israelites to include a variation of the name of the Most High in their children's names. The Hebrew language had no letter "J" in the alphabet and instead utilized the letter "Y" (Lang, 163). Thus, Jacob's name is Ya'qob or Ya'aqov, Joseph is Yosef and Jesus is Yeshua or Yehoshua in Hebrew ("Jacob"; "Joseph"; "Yeshua"). In scripture, we find that the name of

[58]

the Most High God is actually given in Psalm 68:4, *"Sing unto God, sing praises to his name: extol him that rideth upon the heavens by his name JAH, and rejoice before him.* Again, since there was no letter "J" in the Hebrew alphabet, the correct spelling of His name is *"Yah."*

Interestingly, a name search, by typing "Yah" in the Trans-Atlantic Slave Trade Database search box, will reveal hundreds of names containing the word "Yah." It is also interesting to note the increasing number of the young generation of children whose names have the variation of "Yah" in them (e.g., Myah, Aniyah, Saniyah, Aliyah, Kaliyah, Ca'miyah). Given that so many present-day and ancient Hebrew Israelites bear names containing a variation of 'Yah," the scripture in 2 Chronicles 7:14 can seemingly be viewed in a more literal light. *If my people, which are called by my name, shall humble themselves, and pray, and seek my face, and turn from their wicked ways; then will I hear from heaven, and will forgive their sin, and will heal their land.* The discovery of the name of YAH also brings a greater appreciation for why "HalleluYah" ("Hallelujah") is the Highest Praise. Additionally, what of the song, *"Kum Ba Yah"*? The title or phrase "Kum Ba Yah" is said to have been of "African" origin and possibly the earliest version of the song was sung in Gullah, the Creole language spoken by the former slaves living on Georgia and South Carolina's Sea Islands ("Kumbaya").

So there we have it. Based on the scriptural, *archeological* and scholarly evidence reviewed, there should be little doubt that the true Jews are

[59]

none other than the Hebrew Israelites who fell victim to the Transatlantic and Indian Ocean slave trade. They were scattered throughout the four corners of the world *via ships* and sold as *bondmen and bondwomen* just as God forewarned in Deuteronomy 28:64-68. They are now known as African Americans, Jamaicans, Haitians, and Dominicans to name a few. God used the Transatlantic and Indian Ocean slave trade as the vehicle to scatter His Chosen People to the four corners of the Earth, just as He said He would because of their disobedience. The Jews or ancient Hebrew Israelites of the Bible were a Black or dark race of people as both *scriptural* and *archeological* evidence attest, and their physical or bloodline descendants continue to be so today.

Historical evidence supports this fact as well. Ancient Russian icons of the first and second century show biblical Jews and Saints as Black. Ancient drawings in the Catacombs of Rome also show the same. One may even do a simple search on the internet of the first-century Christians and see actual images of ancient saints and Jews of the Bible. The images reveal them to be people of color. Not many icons survived the Byzantine Iconoclastic period. However, black iconic images can be found in the book, *Russian Icons* by Vladimir Ivanov. More resources and access links on this topic are provided in the Suggested Resources section of this book.

So what happened? How did Black or dark-skinned Hebrews Israelite (i.e., Jews) of the Bible become white in color? The answer is through "whitewashing." The Whitewashing of biblical icons took place during the Renaissance period, also known as the Age of Rebirth (Abolitionist). Prior to that time, during the Byzantine era, a number of the biblical icons were iconoclast—that is, literally shattered and destroyed ("Byzantine"). However, again, during the Renaissance period [or **Age of Rebirth**], many of them were "**recreated**" or whitewashed.

The whitewashing of biblical icons was foretold in the book of Maccabees, one of the books of the Apocrypha. The Apocrypha consists of 14 books included in the original 1611 King James Bible between the Old and the New Testaments. For nearly 2,000 years, the Apocrypha was considered part of the Bible before its removal from the King James Version a little more than 100 years ago ("Apocrypha"). Reasons for that removal have been varied and questionable. One reason given for its removal is that the books failed to meet the criteria for canonization. However, if one reviews the criteria for canonization, this reason is suspect and does not hold up to further scrutiny. For example, the criteria for canonization to determine whether a book should be placed in the Bible include whether it was written by a recognized prophet or apostle, thereby having an internal claim of authorship. Is it authentic, truthful, and consistent with other revelation of truth? Was it received, accepted, and used by the early church/believers (Ware)?

These criteria for determining canonization, however, appear to have been inconsistently applied. For instance, several books in the Bible have no internal claim of authorship yet were included in the Bible. These include the book of Judges (author not known; attributed to Samuel by some), Ruth (author unknown; credited to Samuel by some), Esther (author not identified but thought to be Mordecai or one of his contemporaries), Job (author unknown; credited to Moses, Job, and others), Lamentations (author not named; attributed to Jeremiah), and Hebrews (author unknown; attributed to Paul and others), to name a few (Bible Scribes; Lockyer).

Although the Book of Hebrews lacks internal claim to authorship, a justification for its canonization is its faithfulness and/or consistency with other revelations of truth. "Here is where Hebrews shines, in terms of the Church's acceptance of it. Hebrews not only agrees with, but helps explain and bring to greater clarity, what has been taught in the Old Testament" (Ware). However, this same argument (that Hebrews helps to explain and bring greater clarity to what has been taught in scripture) can also apply to many of the books of the Apocrypha. For instance, 1 Maccabees, written in Hebrew by a Jew during the latter part of the 2nd Century, covers the historical period of the Maccabean (Jewish) Revolt against Seleucid rule from 175 to 134. It also records the desecration of the Jerusalem Temple by Antiochus Epiphanes mentioned in the Book of Daniel ("1 Maccabees").

1 Esdras and 2 Esdras. "Esdras" is simply the Greek word for "Ezra," 1 Esdras is a book found in the *Septuagint,* the Greek translation of the Hebrew Bible ("1Esdras"). The Septuagint, which included

[62]

books of the Apocrypha, was the Bible of Greek-speaking Jews in Egypt two centuries before Christ. It later became the Bible of the Jews of the Diaspora and the early Christians (Publisher's, 4). 2 Esdras, is considered one of the gems of apocalyptic literature, consisting of seven visions, including a vision of the heavenly Jerusalem ("2 Esdras"). Its apocalyptic views seem to parallel those of canon scripture.

The Prayer of Manasseh is actually referenced in 2 Chronicles 33:12-13:

> *And when he was in affliction, <u>he besought the LORD his God, and humbled himself greatly before the God of his fathers, And **prayed** unto him</u>: and he was intreated of him, and heard his supplication, and brought him again to Jerusalem into his kingdom. Then Manasseh knew that the LORD he was God.* (Emphasis added)

The Prayer of Manasseh is said to be a prayer from one of Judah's most evil king (see 2 Chronical 33:1-11). The prayer helps one to fully realize and appreciate the Grace of God, who truly does forgive and save anyone who has a repentant heart, no matter what evil things she or he has done:

> <u>O Lord, Almighty God of our fathers, Abraham, Isaac, and Jacob, and of their righteous seed;</u> who hast made heaven and earth, with all the ornament thereof; who hast bound the sea by the word of thy commandment; who hast shut up the deep, and sealed it by thy terrible and glorious name; whom all men fear, and tremble before thy power; for the majesty of thy glory cannot be

borne, and thine angry threatening toward sinners is importable: but thy merciful promise is unmeasurable and unsearchable; for thou art the most high Lord, of great compassion, longsuffering, very merciful, and repentest of the evils of men. Thou, O Lord, according to thy great goodness hast promised repentance and forgiveness to them that have sinned against thee: and of thine infinite mercies hast appointed repentance unto sinners, that they may be saved.

Thou therefore, O Lord, that art the God of the just, hast not appointed repentance to the just, as to Abraham, and Isaac, and Jacob, which have not sinned against thee; but thou hast appointed repentance unto me that am a sinner: for I have sinned above the number of the sands of the sea. My transgressions, O Lord, are multiplied: my transgressions are multiplied, and I am not worthy to behold and see the height of heaven for the multitude of mine iniquities. I am bowed down with many iron bands, that I cannot lift up mine head, neither have any release: for I have provoked thy wrath, and done evil before thee: I did not thy will, neither kept I thy commandments: I have set up abominations, and have multiplied offences. Now therefore I bow the knee of mine heart, beseeching thee of grace. I have sinned, O Lord, I have sinned, and I acknowledge mine iniquities: wherefore, I humbly beseech thee, forgive me, O Lord, forgive me, and destroy me not with mine iniquities. Be not angry with me for ever, by reserving evil for me; neither condemn me to the lower parts of the earth. For thou art the

God, even the God of them that repent; and in me thou wilt shew all thy goodness: for thou wilt save me, that am unworthy, according to thy great mercy. Therefore I will praise thee for ever all the days of my life: for all the powers of the heavens do praise thee, and thine is the glory for ever and ever. Amen. (The Prayer of Mannaseh 1; emphasis added)

Scripture tells us that when Manasseh prayed, God was entreated of him, and heard his supplication, and brought him again to Jerusalem into his kingdom. Then Manasseh knew that the LORD he was God (2 Chron. 33:13). The cited prayer was not found credible for canonization.

The Song of the Three Holy Children, also called The Prayer of Azariah (whose Babylonian name was *Abednego*), is found in the Greek translation of the Hebrew Bible as an addition to the Book of Daniel. Perhaps written about the second or first century BC, the song is found inserted in Daniel 3 right after verse 23: *and these three men, Shadrach, Meshach, and Abednego, fell down bound into the midst of the burning fiery furnace.* Following this verse was "The Song of the Three Holy Children" or "The Prayer of Azariah" [i.e., Abednego] ("Prayer Azariah/Song"). Excerpts of the song are provided below and constitute a hymn of thanksgiving to God for His deliverance of three young men, Ananias, Misael, and Azarias (aka Shadrach, Meshach, and Abednego) from the fiery furnace into which they had been cast.

And they walked in the midst of the fire, praising God, and blessing the Lord. Then

[65]

Azarias [Abednego] stood up, and prayed on this manner; and opening his mouth in the midst of the fire said, Blessed art thou, O Lord God of our fathers: thy name is worthy to be praised and glorified for evermore:... O Ananias [Shadrach], Azarias [Abednego], and Misael [Meshach], bless ye the Lord: praise and exalt him above all for ever: far he hath delivered us from hell, and saved us from the hand of death, and delivered us out of the midst of the furnace and burning flame: even out of the midst of the fire hath he delivered us. O give thanks unto the Lord, because he is gracious: for his mercy endureth for ever. O all ye that worship the Lord, bless the God of gods, praise him, and give him thanks: for his mercy endureth for ever. ("Prayer of Azariah [Abednego]")

Additional arguments as to why the books of Apocrypha were not considered authoritative scripture are because the early Jewish believers never accepted them and neither the apostles or Jesus ever cited them in the New Testament. However, Ignatius of Antioch 35-107 AD, a student of the Apostle John, used the Septuagint and quoted often from the Old Testament, including the Apocrypha (Davis). Additionally, J.N.D Kelly in his book *Early Christian Doctrines-Revised* cites several other Church Fathers who quoted from the Apocrypha. As mentioned earlier, the Septuagint—the Greek translation of the Hebrew Bible, included the books of the Apocrypha and was the Bible of Greek-speaking Jews in Egypt two centuries before

Christ. It later became the Bible of the Jews of the Diaspora and the early Christians (Publisher's, 4).

To reiterate, one other argument why the books of the Apocrypha were not considered authoritative or "God-Inspired" is because none of them is quoted by the Apostles or by Jesus/Yehoshua in the New Testament. Proponents of this argument point out that, if either Jesus/Yehoshua or the apostles considered the Apocrypha to be scripture, they would have referred to them in some way. There are certain *non-apocryphal* books that *are* cited in scripture, such as the Book of Enoch (Jude 4,6,13,14, 15) and the Book of Jasher (Joshua 10:13 and 2 Samuel 1:18) however, and were never included in the Bible. One might wonder why these books were never included in the Bible since certain writers of the Bible recognized them in *their* writings. By the same token, there are *several* Old Testament books that *are not* quoted in the New Testament by the apostles or Jesus/Yehoshua, such as Ezra, Nehemiah, Esther, Song of Solomon, Lamentations, Obadiah, and Nahum. Does this mean that these books too, were not inspired writings? As you may recall, the Book of Esther was neither quoted in the New Testament nor did it have an internal claim of authorship. Yet, despite not meeting these criteria, it was found worthy of canonization.

Finally, it should be noted that Apocryphal books *are* of Jewish origin (Publisher's, 3). Fragments from the Dead Sea Scrolls, dating back to before 70 AD, contained parts of the Apocrypha books in Hebrew that include Tobit and Sirach

("Apocrypha"). The bottom line is this: One can debate until the cows come home whether these books are worthy of authoritative honor or hold any merit within themselves. The proof, however, is always in the pudding. Therefore, one should read and judge for one's self whether these books are good for edification and provide more insight into known read books of the Bible. You may well come to agree with Martin Luther that the books of the Apocrypha are not on the same level or equal to the Holy Scriptures of the Bible and yet are useful and good for reading. At least you will have drawn your own conclusion on the matter and not mine or someone else's. My advice in all things is to be led by the Holy Spirit to discern what is and is not truth.

Nonetheless, returning to the topic at hand, the whitewashing of Black biblical icons took place during the Renaissance period and was foretold in the Apocrypha book of I Maccabees 3:48 which reads. *"And laide open the booke of the Law, wherein the heathen had sought to paint the likeness of their images."* The false images of Jesus/Yehoshua seen in churches throughout the world are purportedly painted in the likeness of the son of Pope Alexander VI, Cesare Borgia. Cesare was the favorite and illegitimate son of the Pope who many in his day believed had an incestuous relationship with his sister. He fathered at least 11 illegitimate children. He was also suspected in his day of having his older brother assassinated to obtain the coveted position as Captain General of the military forces of the papacy held by his brother. During the time when the Roman Catholic Church waged war against Islam, Leonardo Di Vinci was commissioned by the Pope to paint or recast icons of Christ in the image of his beloved son, Cesare ("False Image"). This falsification of the image of Christ was also foretold in an Apocrypha book, The Wisdom of Solomon.

> For a father afflicted with untimely mourning, when he hath made an image of his child soon taken away, now honoured him as a god, which was then a dead man, and delivered to those that were under him ceremonies and sacrifices. Thus in process of time an ungodly custom grown strong was kept as a law, and graven images were worshipped by the commandments of kings. Whom men could not honour in presence, because they dwelt far off, they took the counterfeit of his visage from far, and made an express image of a king whom they honoured, to the end that by this their forwardness they might flatter him that was absent, as if he were present. Also the singular diligence of the artificer did help to set forward the ignorant to more superstition. For he, peradventure willing to please one in authority, forced all his skill to make the resemblance of the best fashion. And so the multitude, allured by the grace of the work, took him now for a god, which a little before was but honoured. And this was an occasion to deceive the world: for men, serving either calamity or tyranny, did ascribe unto stones and stocks the incommunicable name." (Wisd. of Sol. 4.15-21)

In First Corinthians, it is written, "*Doth not even nature itself teach you, that, if a man have long hair, it is a shame unto him?"* (1 Corinthians 11:14; emphasis added). Based on this scripture, it is not likely that Jesus/Yehoshua had long hair. Nor is it likely that he had straight hair or fair/white skin, being of the Tribe of Judah and thus a "Jew" after the flesh (Heb. 7:14; Rev. 5:5; Matt. 2:2; Rev. 1:14-15). Thus, the image that most people have of what Jesus/Yehoshua looks like is false. The Book of the Wisdom of Solomon also sums up quite effectively the effects of whitewashing Black biblical icons and the image of Jesus//Yehoshua, *"For the planning of painting idols was the starting of spiritual fornication, and the invention of them the corruption of life"* (14:12; emphasis added). In essence, the remaking or the repainting of the biblical icons and the image of Christ into "their own image and likeness" was the making of themselves idol gods.

The Book of the Wisdom of Solomon also alludes to how surprised *"the heathen"* will be when it is revealed that Blacks or the once-called Negros are the true Jews or "Chosen People of God":

> Then shall the righteous man stand in great boldness before the face of such as have afflicted him, <u>and made no account of his labours</u>. When they see it, they shall be troubled with terrible fear, and shall be amazed at the strangeness of his salvation, so far beyond all that they looked for. And they repenting and groaning for anguish of spirit shall say within themselves, <u>This was he, whom we had sometimes in derision, and a proverb of reproach: We fools accounted his life madness, and his end to be without honour:</u>

[70]

How is he numbered among the children of God, and his lot is among the saints! Therefore have we erred from the way of truth, and the light of righteousness hath not shined unto us, and the sun of righteousness rose not upon us. We wearied ourselves in the way of wickedness and destruction: yea, we have gone through deserts, where there lay no way: but as for the way of the Lord, we have not known it. What hath pride profited us? or what good hath riches with our vaunting brought us? All those things are passed away like a shadow, and as a post that hasted by... (Wis. of Sol. 5:2-9; emphasis added)

Of great shame, the practice of whitewashing continues today. It is evident in the "whitewashing" of the Ancient Egyptians, especially the Ancient Egyptian Pharaohs, despite archeological proof to the contrary.

I now pose this question. If Indo-Europeans have retained their skin color to this present day, whose genealogy can be traced back to Noah's son Japheth, if Africans and many Egyptians have retained their dark skin color to this present day, whose genealogy can be traced back to Noah's son Ham, why is it so hard to believe that the Hebrew Israelites, the true Jews have *also* retained their physical appearance (i.e. dark skin color), whose genealogy can be traced back to Noah's son Shem, the progenitor of the Semitic race? As pointed out earlier, there is now genetic data that support scriptural, historical, and archeological evidence as to who the true Jews are and are not today. For instance, a number of DNA studies on the Black

[71]

Lemba Tribe of South Africa regarding their Hebrew or Jewish roots have been done. For a list of DNA research of this nature, please refer to the Suggested Resource section of this book. As pointed our earlier, DNA testing has also shown that the Ashkenazi "Jews" occupying the land of Israel today are not physical or bloodline descendants of Abraham, Isaac, and Jacob. They are **European** "Jews" or Gentiles, as scripture indicates, being the physical descendants of Noah's son Japheth and NOT descendants of Shem, Abraham, Isaac, and Jacob (Gen. 10:1-5). Please see again, the Suggested Resource section for a list of sources on this topic.

Forgetting their heritage and/or identity, was part of the curse for the Children of Israel's repetitive disobedience to God.

> *And thou, even thyself, shalt discontinue from thine heritage that I gave thee; and I will cause thee to serve thine enemies <u>in the land which thou knowest not</u>: for ye have kindled a fire in mine anger, which shall burn for ever.* (Jer.17:4; emphasis added)

The first thing the slave masters did was take away the enslaved Hebrew Israelites' names, just as was done to their ancestors in their Babylonian Captivity. The slave master also forbade them to learn how to read or write. They then told them *their* version of who the enslaved Hebrew Israelites was and taught them a distorted "gospel" accompanied by a false physical image of Christ.

The ox knoweth his owner, and the ass his master's crib: <u>but Israel doth not know, my people doth not consider.</u> Ah sinful nation, a people laden with iniquity, a seed of evildoers, children that are corrupters: <u>they have forsaken the LORD, they have provoked the Holy One of Israel unto anger, they are gone away backward.</u> (Isa. 1:3-4)

*Yea, the stork in the heaven <u>knoweth her appointed times;</u> and the turtle and the crane and the swallow observe the time of their coming; <u>but my people **know not** the judgment of the LORD.</u>* (Jer. 8:7; emphasis added)

<u>For the LORD hath poured out upon you the spirit of deep sleep, and hath closed your eyes</u>: the prophets and your rulers, the seers hath he covered. (Isa. 29:10; emphasis added)

*What then? Israel hath not obtained that which he seeketh for; but the election hath obtained it, and the rest were blinded. <u>(According as it is written, **God hath given them the spirit of slumber, eyes that they should not see, and ears that they should not hear;**) unto this day.</u> And David saith, Let their <u>table be made a snare, and a trap, and a stumblingblock, and a recompence unto them: Let their eyes be darkened, that they may not see</u>, and bow down their back always.* (Rom. 11:7-10; emphasis added)

For I would not, brethren, that ye should be ignorant of this mystery, lest ye should be wise in your own conceits; <u>that blindness in part is happened to Israel, until the fullness of the Gentiles be come in.</u> (Rom. 11:25; emphasis added)

[73]

According to scripture, the *partial blindness* that has happened to Israel will last "*until the fullness of the Gentiles come in.*" Scripture also tells us that **in the meantime** or during the time of Israel's partial blindness, *Jerusalem* shall *be trodden down of the Gentiles, until the times of the Gentiles* [i.e. the time of Gentile domination] *be fulfilled* (Luke 21:24). Israel will also be *swallowed up and be wanderers among the Gentiles* just as they were in the days of their Assyrian captivity (Hos. 8:8; Hos. 9:17). *With stammering lips,* of *another* or a *foreign tongue,* God will speak to His Chosen people (Isa. 28:11). These scriptures help explain why the land of Israel is presently occupied by Gentiles who say they are Jews but are not and why the physical descendants of Jacob at large are lost to their identity and basically living as *wanderers* or in obscurity, *swallowed up by the Gentiles.* The scriptures also help explain why the "gospel" at large, is being taught to Hebrew Israelites by Gentiles in a *foreign unskilled tongue* when God had entrusted His Chosen People to be the carriers and witnesses of His Word and truth to all nations.

It must be remembered, however, that, with respect to His Chosen People, *God Himself* providentially did or allowed the scattering of Israel among the nations appointed. The scattering was also done at **His appointed time**, by **His appointed method** (i.e., via ships) and according to **His appointed Judgment**—sold as bondmen and bondwomen to these nations because of their disobedience to Him.

[74]

*And the LORD shall scatter thee among all people, from the one end of the earth even unto the other; and there thou shalt serve other gods, which neither thou nor thy fathers have known, even wood and stone... And the Lord shall bring thee into Egypt **again** with ships, by the way whereof I spake unto thee, Thou shalt see it no more again: and there ye shall be sold unto your enemies for bondmen and bondwomen, and no man shall buy you.* (Deut. 28:64, 68; emphasis added)

Who gave Jacob for a spoil, and Israel to the robbers? did not the LORD, he against whom we have sinned? for they would not walk in his ways, neither were they obedient unto his law. Therefore he hath poured upon him the fury of his anger, and the strength of battle: and it hath set him on fire round about, yet he knew not; and it burned him, yet he laid it not to heart. (Isa. 42:24-25; emphasis added)

... for I have wounded thee with the wound of an enemy, with the chastisement of a cruel one, for the multitude of thine iniquity; because thy sins were increased. Why criest thou for thine affliction? thy sorrow is incurable for the multitude of thine iniquity: because thy sins were increased, I have done these things unto thee. (Jer. 30:14-15; emphasis added)

Hear the word of the LORD, O ye nations, and declare it in the isles afar off, and say, He that scattered Israel will gather him, and keep him, as a shepherd doth his flock. (Jer. 31:10; emphasis added)

And I will set my glory among the heathen, and all the heathen shall see my judgment that I have executed, and my hand that I have laid upon them. So the house of Israel shall know that I am the LORD their God from that day and forward. And the heathen shall know that the house of Israel went into captivity for their iniquity: because they trespassed against me, therefore hid I my face from them, and gave them into the hand of their enemies: so fell they all by the sword. According to their uncleanness and according to their transgressions have I done unto them, and hid my face from them. (Ezek. 39:21-24; emphasis added)

Thus, it was **God** who scattered His People and it is **He** who will regather and redeem them from the nations to which He scattered them. He will also be the one who brings them back to the land of Israel as He promised their forefathers. It will not be by any organization but by God Himself. He, alone, will bring His people back to their promised land of "Yisrael."

And it shall come to pass in that day, that the Lord shall set his hand again the second time to recover the remnant of his people, which shall be left, from Assyria, and from Egypt, and from Pathros, and from Cush, and from Elam, and from Shinar, and from Hamath, and from the islands of the sea. And he shall set up an ensign for the nations, and shall assemble the outcasts of Israel, and gather together the dispersed of Judah from the four corners of the earth. (Isa. 11:11-12; emphasis added)

Therefore say, Thus saith the Lord GOD; I will even gather you from the people, and assemble you out of the countries where ye have been scattered, and I will give you the land of Israel. (Ezek. 11:17; emphasis added)

Therefore thus saith the Lord GOD; Now will I bring again the captivity of Jacob, and have mercy upon the whole house of Israel, and will be jealous for my holy name; After that they have borne their shame, and all their trespasses whereby they have trespassed against me, when they dwelt safely in their land, and none made them afraid. When I have brought them again from the people, and gathered them out of their enemies' lands, and am sanctified in them in the sight of many nations; Then shall they know that I am the LORD their God, which caused them to be led into captivity among the heathen.... (Ezek. 39:25-28; emphasis added)

Thus speaketh the LORD God of Israel, saying, Write thee all the words that I have spoken unto thee in a book. For, lo, the days come, saith the LORD, that I will bring again the captivity of my people Israel and Judah, saith the LORD: and I will cause them to return to the land that I gave to their fathers, and they shall possess it. (Jer. 30:2-3; emphasis added)

*Therefore, behold, the days come, saith the LORD, that they shall no more say, The LORD liveth, which brought up the children of Israel out of the land of Egypt; BUT, The LORD liveth, which brought up and which led the **SEED** of the House of Israel out of the north country, AND from ALL COUNTRIES whither I had **driven** them; and they shall dwell in their own land.* (Jer. 23:7-8; emphasis added)

[77]

Thus saith the LORD of hosts; Behold, I will save my people from the east country, and from the west country; And I will bring them, and they shall dwell in the midst of Jerusalem: and they shall be my people, and I will be their God, in truth and in righteousness. (Zech.8:7-8; emphasis added)

Yes, God Himself will regather His Chosen People back to their promised land. Thus, He has not forgotten Israel nor has He cast them off forever or replaced them with the "Church." Though, as promised, He made *the remembrance of them to cease among men* and they have been discontinued from their inheritance due to their disobedience, in the last days, God will show recompense to Israel and bring full retribution to all nations on behalf of His Chosen ones.

And the LORD thy God will bring thee into the land which thy fathers possessed, and thou shalt possess it; and he will do thee good, and multiply thee above thy fathers. And the LORD thy God will circumcise thine heart, and the heart of thy seed, to love the LORD thy God with all thine heart, and with all thy soul, that thou mayest live. And the LORD thy God will put all these curses upon thine enemies, and on them that hate thee, which persecuted thee. (Deut. 30:5-7; emphasis added)

Hear the word of the Lord, O ye nations, and declare it in the isles afar off, and say, He that scattered Israel will gather him, and keep him, as a shepherd doth his flock. For the Lord hath redeemed Jacob, and ransomed him from the hand of him that was stronger than he.

[78]

Therefore they shall come and sing in the height of Zion, and shall flow together to the goodness of the Lord, for wheat, and for wine, and for oil, and for the young of the flock and of the herd: and their soul shall be as a watered garden; <u>and they shall not sorrow any more at all</u>. Then shall the virgin rejoice in the dance, both young men and old together: <u>for I will turn their mourning into joy, and will comfort them, and make them rejoice from their sorrow</u>. And I will satiate the soul of the priests with fatness, and my people shall be satisfied with my goodness, saith the Lord... <u>And it shall come to pass, that like as I have watched over them, to pluck up, and to break down, and to throw down, and to destroy, and to afflict; so will I watch over them, to build, and to plant, saith the Lord.</u> (Jer. 31:10-14, 28; emphasis added)

*Alas! for that day is great, so that none is like it: it is even the time of <u>Jacob's trouble</u> but he shall be saved out of it. For it shall come to pass in that day, saith the LORD of hosts, <u>that I will break his yoke from off thy neck, and will burst thy bonds, and strangers shall no more serve themselves of him</u>: But they shall serve the LORD their God, and David their king, whom I will raise up unto them. Therefore <u>fear thou not</u>, O my servant Jacob, saith the LORD; <u>neither be dismayed, O Israel: for, lo, I will save thee FROM AFAR, and THY SEED from the land of THEIR CAPTIVITY; and Jacob shall return, and shall be in rest, and be quiet, and **none shall make him afraid**</u>.* (Jer.30:7-10; emphasis added)

Thus saith the LORD; Behold, <u>I will</u> bring <u>again</u> the captivity of Jacob's tents, and have mercy on his dwelling places; and the city shall be builded upon her own heap, and the palace shall remain after the manner thereof. And out of them shall proceed thanksgiving and the voice of them that make merry: and <u>I will</u> multiply them, and they shall not be few; <u>I will</u> also glorify them, and they shall not be small. Their children also shall be as aforetime, and their congregation shall be established before me, and <u>I will</u> punish all that oppress them. And their nobles shall be of themselves, and their governor shall proceed from the midst of them; and <u>I will</u> cause him to draw near, and he shall approach unto me: for who is this that engaged his heart to approach unto me? saith the LORD. And ye shall be my people, and <u>I will</u> be your God. Behold, the whirlwind of the LORD goeth forth with fury, a continuing whirlwind: it shall fall with pain upon the head of the wicked. The fierce anger of the LORD shall not return, until he hath done it, and until he have performed the intents of his heart: <u>in the latter days ye shall consider it.</u>
(Jer. 30:18-24; emphasis added)

Thus saith the Lord GOD; When I shall have gathered the house of Israel <u>from the people among whom they are scattered</u>, and shall be sanctified in them in the sight of the heathen, <u>then</u> shall they dwell in their land that I have given to my servant Jacob. And they shall dwell <u>safely therein</u>, and shall build houses, and plant vineyards; yea, they shall dwell with confidence, <u>when I</u> have executed judgments <u>upon all those that despise them</u> round about

[80]

them; and they shall know that I am the LORD their God. (Ezek. 28:25-26; emphasis added)

And say unto them, Thus saith the Lord GOD; Behold, I will take the children of Israel from among the heathen, whither they be gone, and will gather them on every side, and bring them into their OWN land: And I will make them ONE NATION in the land UPON THE MOUNTAINS OF ISRAEL ; and one king shall be king to them all: and they shall be no more two nations, neither shall they be divided into two kingdoms any more at all. Neither shall they defile themselves any more with their idols, nor with their detestable things, nor with any of their transgressions: but I will save them out of all their dwelling places, wherein they have sinned, and will cleanse them: so shall they be my people, and I will be their God. (Ezek.37:21-23; emphasis added)

*Behold, at that time I will undo all that afflict thee: and I will save her that halteth, and gather her that was driven out; and I will get them praise and fame in every land where they have been put to shame. At that time will I bring you again, even in the time that I gather you: for I will make you a name and praise among all people of the earth, **when** I turn back your captivity before your eyes, saith the LORD.* (Zeph. 3:19-20; emphasis added)

And I will bring again the captivity of my people of Israel, and they shall build the waste cities, and inhabit them; and they shall plant vineyards, and drink the wine thereof; they shall also make gardens, and eat the fruit of them. (Amos 9: 14; emphasis added)

[81]

And it shall come to pass in that day, that the remnant of Israel, and such as are escaped of the house of Jacob, shall no more again stay [rely] upon him that smote them; but shall stay [rely] upon the Lord, the Holy One of Israel, in truth. (Isa. 10:20)

*For, behold, in those days, and in that time, when I shall bring **again** the captivity of Judah and Jerusalem, I will also gather all nations, and will bring them down into the valley of Jehoshaphat, and will plead with them there for my people and for my heritage Israel, whom they have scattered among the nations, and parted my land. And they have cast lots for my people; and have given a boy for a harlot, and sold a girl for wine, that they might drink.* (Joel 3:1-3)

Multitudes, multitudes in the valley of decision: for the day of the LORD is near in the valley of decision. The sun and the moon shall be darkened, and the stars shall withdraw their shining. The LORD also shall roar out of Zion, and utter his voice from Jerusalem; and the heavens and the earth shall shake: but the LORD will be the hope of his people, and the strength of the children of Israel. So shall ye know that I am the LORD your God dwelling in Zion, my holy mountain: then shall Jerusalem be holy, and there shall no strangers pass through her any more... Egypt shall be a desolation, and Edom shall be a desolate wilderness, for the violence against the children of Judah, because they have shed innocent blood in their land. But Judah shall dwell for ever, and Jerusalem from generation to generation. For I will cleanse their blood

[82]

that I have not cleansed: for the LORD dwelleth in Zion. (Joel 3:14-17; 19-21; emphasis added)

From beyond the rivers of Ethiopia my suppliants, even the daughter of my dispersed, shall bring mine offering... Behold, <u>at that time</u> I will undo all that afflict thee: and I <u>will save her that halteth, and gather her that was driven out; and I will get them praise and fame in every land where they have been put to shame.</u> .At that time <u>will I bring you again, even in the time that I gather you: for I will make you a name and a praise among all people of the earth, when I turn back your captivity before your eyes,</u> saith the LORD. (Zeph. 3:10, 19-20; emphasis added)

And so all Israel shall be saved: as it is written, There shall come out of Sion the Deliverer, and shall turn away ungodliness from Jacob: <u>for this is my covenant unto them,</u> when I shall take away their sins. (Rom.11:26–27; emphasis added)

Future Glory of Israel (Isaiah 60)

Arise, shine; for thy light is come, and the glory of the LORD is risen upon thee. For, behold, the darkness shall cover the earth, and gross darkness the people: <u>but the LORD shall arise upon thee, and his glory shall be seen upon thee.</u> And the Gentiles shall come to thy light, and kings to the brightness of thy rising. Lift up thine eyes round about, and see: all they gather themselves together, they come to thee: thy sons shall come from far, and thy daughters shall be nursed at thy side. Then *thou shalt see, and flow together, and thine heart shall fear, and be enlarged; because the abundance of the sea shall be converted unto thee, <u>the forces of the Gentiles shall come unto thee</u>. The multitude of camels shall cover thee, the dromedaries of Midian and Ephah; all they from Sheba shall come: they shall bring gold and incense; and they shall shew forth the praises of the LORD. All the flocks of Kedar shall be gathered together unto thee, the rams of Nebaioth shall minister unto thee: they shall come up with acceptance on mine altar, and I will glorify the house of my glory.*

Who are these that fly as a cloud, and as the doves to their windows? Surely the isles shall wait for me, and the ships of Tarshish first, to bring thy sons from far, their silver and their gold with them, unto the name of the LORD thy God, and to the Holy One of Israel, because he hath glorified thee. <u>And the sons of strangers shall build up thy walls, and their kings shall minister unto thee</u>: for in my wrath I smote thee, but in my favour have I had mercy on thee. Therefore thy gates shall be open continually; they shall not be shut day nor night; <u>that men may bring unto thee the forces of the Gentiles</u>, and that their kings may be brought. <u>For the nation and kingdom that will not serve thee shall perish; yea, those nations shall be utterly wasted.</u> The glory of Lebanon shall come unto thee, the fir tree, the pine tree, and the box together, to beautify the place of my sanctuary; and I will make the place of my feet glorious. <u>The sons also of them that afflicted thee shall come bending unto thee; and all they that despised thee shall bow</u>

themselves down at the soles of thy feet; and
they shall call thee; The city of the LORD, The
Zion of the Holy One of Israel. Whereas thou
has been forsaken and hated, so that no man
went through thee, I will make thee an eternal
excellency, a joy of many generations.

Thou shalt also suck the milk of the Gentiles,
and shalt suck the breast of kings: and thou
shalt know that I the LORD am thy Saviour and
thy Redeemer, the mighty One of Jacob. For
brass I will bring gold, and for iron I will
bring silver, and for wood brass, and for
stones iron: I will also make thy officers peace,
and thine exactors righteousness. Violence
shall no more be heard in thy land, wasting
nor destruction within thy borders; but thou
shalt call thy walls Salvation, and thy gates
Praise. The sun shall be no more thy light by
day; neither for brightness shall the moon give
light unto thee: but the LORD shall be unto thee
an everlasting light, and thy God thy glory. Thy
sun shall no more go down; neither shall thy
moon withdraw itself: for the LORD shall be
thine everlasting light, and the days of thy
mourning shall be ended. Thy people also shall
be all righteous: they shall inherit the land for
ever, the branch of my planting, the work of my
hands, that I may be glorified. A little one shall
become a thousand, and a small one a strong
nation: I the LORD will hasten it in his time.
(Emphasis added)

Although God's Chosen People are currently
living in obscurity, swallowed up by the Gentiles,
largely not knowing their true heritage or who they
are, the Bible does speak of a great awakening that

will take place among His people. This Great Awakening into their identity will take place in the last days, followed by a collective cry of repentance on their part. Not only do the scriptures speak of such an awakening taking place, but even seem to indicate that Israel's restoration and Jesus/ Yehoshua's return is predicated upon such an awakening and *collective* repentance on the part of His People, Israel.

> *And it <u>SHALL</u> come to pass, when all these things are come upon thee, <u>the blessing and the curse</u>, which I have set before thee, and thou <u>SHALT CALL THEM to mind AMONG ALL the nations,</u> whither <u>the LORD thy God hath driven thee</u>, And shalt <u>RETURN</u> unto the LORD thy God, and shalt <u>OBEY</u> his voice according to all that I command thee <u>this</u> day, THOU and THY CHILDREN, with all thine heart, and with all thy soul; That **THEN** the LORD thy God will TURN THY CAPTIVITY, and have compassion upon thee, and WILL RETURN and GATHER thee from ALL the NATIONS, whither the LORD thy God hath scattered thee.* (Deut. 30:1–3; emphasis added)

This scripture suggests that God knew the Children of Israel would not keep His covenant and therefore would inevitably incur upon themselves both the blessings and the curses of the covenant found in Deuteronomy 28. This scripture also seems to indicate that the Children of Israel would inevitably come to call the *blessings and curses to mind, <u>among all the nations where the Lord God hath scattered them</u>*. This is currently taking place as Hebrew Israelites *are now* beginning to call to

[86]

mind the blessing and the curses of Deuteronomy in every nation where they have been scattered. It is not enough to awaken, however, to their true heritage as "God's Chosen People" and bloodline descendants of Jacob, (though that will be a major feat in itself), *they and their children* must also **RETURN** unto the Lord. *"Obey His voice in all that He commanded them and their forefathers and do so with all their heart and soul."* **THEN**, the Lord will *TURN THEIR CAPTIVITY* and have compassion upon them. *HE WILL RETURN and GATHER THEM* from all the nations, whither He hath scattered them. Thus, Israel's deliverance from *their present day captivity and exile* is dependent upon an awakening unto their true heritage or identity, **followed** by a collective repentance as a people and a RETURN unto the Most High God.

Israel's *last and final* restoration will be consistent with that of her biblical history. Historically, the Children of Israel sinned against God. He allowed them to go into captivity as a judgment against them. He later restored them but only *after* they had repented for their disobedience and RETURNED to Him *as a people*. Only then, did He deliver them from their captivities and restore them to their land. Thus, in His Word, God set forth *specific and necessary conditions* that Israel had to meet before He restored them from the land of their captivities—an acknowledgement of sin, repentance for sin, and a RETURN unto Him, the God of Israel. These conditions are noted in the following passages of scripture.

[87]

If they sin against thee... and thou be angry with them, and deliver them to the enemy, so that they carry them away captives unto the land of the enemy, far or near; <u>*Yet if they shall bethink themselves* **in the land whither they were carried captives,** **and repent,** **and make supplication unto thee** *in the land of them that carried them captives, saying,* *We have sinned, and have done perversely, we have committed wickedness;*</u> *And so* **return** *unto thee* <u>*with all their heart, and with all their soul, in the land of their enemies, which led them away captive, and pray unto thee.*</u> **Then** *hear thou their prayer and their supplication in heaven thy dwelling place,* <u>*and maintain their cause,*</u> *And forgive thy people that have sinned against thee, and all their transgressions wherein they have transgressed against thee, and give them compassion before them who carried them captive, that they may have compassion on them.* <u>*For they be thy people, and thine inheritance...*</u> (1Kings 8:46-51; emphasis added)

<u>*If they shall confess their iniquity, and the iniquity of their fathers,*</u> *with their trespass which they trespassed against me,* <u>*and that also they have walked* **contrary** *unto me;* *And that I also have walked contrary unto them,*</u> *and have brought them into the land of their enemies;* <u>*if then their uncircumcised hearts be humbled, and they then accept of the punishment of their iniquity:* **Then** *will I remember my covenant with Jacob, and also my covenant with Isaac, and also my covenant with Abraham will I remember; and I will*</u>

[88]

remember the land. (Lev. 26:40-42; emphasis added)

Again, in His Word, God hath set forth conditions that Israel had to meet **before** He restored them from the lands of their captivities (1Kings 8:46-51, Lev. 26:40-42; Deut. 30:1-3). Given the **scriptural** conditions for Israel's restoration and final return to their land, one might ask whether the current State of Israel is a fulfillment of scripture and Bible prophecy (Davies). Based on the scriptural conditions necessary for Israel's restoration and return to their promised land, one has to surmise that it is not. Scripture tells us that **God Himself** will do the regathering of His people back to their land. It will not be by man's ingenuity or by an organization, but by God Himself (Duet. 30:1-3; Jer.30:1-3, 10, 18; Jer. 31:10-11; Isa. 11:11-12; Isa. 27:12; Isa. 43:5-6; Zech. 8:7-8; Zeph. 3:19-20; Ezek. 11:17; Ezek. 39:25-28; Ezek. 37:21-28). The current State of Israel exists today as a result of political maneuvering and manipulation on the part of man (i.e. the Balfour Declaration) and not by the very hand of God. Scripture also tells us that, when God regathers His people back to their land, they will *be at rest and in quiet and none shall make him afraid.* (Jer.30:10). However, since the forming of the State of Israel, this has not been the case. The land instead has been full of nothing but unrest, wars, turmoil, and fear.

Though the European Jews claim they have been "*restored*" to the land of Israel, one has to ask how this can be, if they are the true descendants of the Biblical Israelites. Remember, Isaiah 42:22 said that Israel *"is a people robbed and spoiled,"* *"snared in holes,"* and *"hid in prison houses."* Further, *"none delivereth"* and *"none say, Restore"* ("More Curses & Prophesies"). In other words, NO ONE or NO MAN will plead Israel's cause to repair, *liberate* or RESTORE them. Also, God says of Israel in Jeremiah 30:12-13 that Israel's *bruise is incurable* and her wound, *grievous*, that there is *"NONE TO PLEAD"* her cause that she may be *bound up* and she has *no healing medicines."* Thus God will permit NO MAN or NO ONE to liberate, deliver, or HEAL Israel, save Himself. *"For I will restore health unto thee, and I will heal thee of thy wounds, saith the LORD; because <u>they called thee an Outcast</u>, saying, This is Zion, whom <u>no man seeketh after</u>."* (Jer. 30:17; emphasis added)

Furthermore, the Jews or Hebrew Israelites can't be in the land of Israel as a *sovereign* nation when Jesus/Yehoshua returns because, according to scripture, Israel will still be in the land of their captivity in all the nations where God has scattered them while in the meantime the Holy city of Jerusalem *is trodden down by the Gentiles until the times of the Gentiles be fulfilled* (Luke 21:24; "More Curses & Prophesies"). Hosea 8:8 and Hosea 9:17 further convey where Israel will be in the latter days.

> *Israel is swallowed up; <u>now</u> shall they be among the Gentiles as a vessel wherein is no pleasure.* (Hos. 8:8; emphasis added).

> *My God will cast them away, because they did not harken unto him: <u>and they shall be</u>*

wanderers among the nations. (Hos. 9:17; emphasis added)

Thus, until the Messiah returns, the remnant of Israel will be *among the Gentiles in the midst of many people, swallowed up among the Gentiles* and *wanderers among the nations*—not in the land of Israel as a Sovereign Nation. Furthermore, the establishment of the Jewish State of Israel in 1948 *does not* fulfill the Dry Bones prophecy of Ezekiel 37 but rather fulfils Genesis 9:27 and Luke 21:24.

A particular passage of scripture that is often cited that causes some to believe that European "Jews" actually are the "true Jews" is Zechariah 12:10. However, almost *inevitably* when Zechariah 12:10 is quoted a commentary like this one immediately follows, "When they behold the one whom they have pierced they shall mourn *and shall ask for and/or receive Salvation*." However, when this scripture is read in context with the verses that follow, no such thing is mentioned or takes place. When Zechariah 12:10 is misinterpreted in this manner, it would seem to give credence to the supposition that the current European "Jews" are presently ignorant or "blind" to who the Messiah truly is and whose eyes will be opened leading to repentance upon seeing Him at His second coming. At *that* point and time, all European "Jews" would be saved. However, let's go back and read Zechariah 12:10 along with the verses that follow to get the accurate interpretation of this scripture. First, let's lay the ground work by referring to earlier verses in Zechariah where God says **He** will bring His people back to Jerusalem.

[91]

*Thus saith the LORD of hosts; Behold, I will save my people from the east country, and from the west country; And I will bring them, and they shall dwell in the midst of Jerusalem: and they shall be my people, and I will be their God, in truth and in righteousness.... And it shall come to pass, that **as ye were a curse among the heathen, O house of Judah, and house of Israel**; so will I save you, and ye shall be a blessing: fear not, but let your hands be strong. For thus saith the Lord of hosts; As* I thought to punish you, when your fathers provoked me to wrath, *saith the Lord of hosts, and I repented not:* So again have I thought in these days to do well unto Jerusalem and to the house of Judah: fear ye not. *(Zech. 8:7-8, 13-15; emphasis added)*

And I will strengthen the house of Judah, and I will save the house of Joseph, and I will bring them again to place them; for I have mercy upon them: and they shall be as though I had not cast them off: for I am the LORD their God, and will hear them. (Zech. 10:6)

In that day will I make the governors of Judah like an hearth of fire among the wood, and like a torch of fire in a sheaf; and they shall devour all the people round about, on the right hand and on the left: and Jerusalem shall be inhabited again in her own place, even in Jerusalem. (Zech. 12:6)

And it shall come to pass in that day, that I will seek to destroy all the nations that come against Jerusalem. And I will pour upon the house of David, and upon the inhabitants of Jerusalem, the spirit of grace and of

supplications: and they shall look upon me
whom they have pierced, and they shall mourn
for him, as one mourneth for his only son, and
shall be in bitterness for him, as one that is in
bitterness for his firstborn. In that day shall
there be a great mourning in Jerusalem, as the
mourning of Hadadrimmon in the valley of
Megiddon. And the land shall mourn, every
family apart; the family of the house of David
apart, and their wives apart; the family of the
house of Nathan apart, and their wives apart.
The family of the house of Levi apart, and their
wives apart; the family of Shimei apart, and
their wives apart; All the families that remain,
every family apart, and their wives apart.
(Zech. 12:9-14)

Thus, when the children of Israel look upon the one whom they have pierced, they go into a national mourning over what they have done. Salvation is not in play here. A FULL RECOGNITION of a swept-over hideous sin is at play here.

Thus, the children or the Nation of Israel mourn over the terrible deed they did to the Messiah once the cruelty and shame of their action is FULLY realized. Only when they fully realize it do they then mourn in GREAT SORROW or in bitterness of heart and in repentance as a Nation for the FIRST TIME EVER over what they did, especially after the Most High pours out his *spirit of grace and supplications* upon them, enabling them to do so. There IS no crying out for salvation here. There IS no **sudden** recognition of the Messiah as the Messiah. There is, however, an awakening to the full extent of the CRUELTY and SHAME in having

[93]

the Messiah crucified, followed by a bitterness of sorrow and a repentance NATIONALLY for such an act. EACH FAMILY APART grieves. A NATIONAL grieving is needed; a NATIONAL grieving is required; and a National grieving is finally SUPPLIED.

Additionally, with respect to the **European** Jews fitting Bible prophecy, God said He would cause the Children of Israel to *serve* their enemies that **He** would send against them in *Hunger,* in *Thirst,* in *Nakedness* and in *Want of All Things* (Deut. 28:48). Where are the European "Jews" lacking in ANYTHING? They own or control practically everything—the media outlets, mass communication networks, Hollywood, world banks and Corporations, and I suspect the Legal/Prison systems (i.e., a modern day form of slavery, as nothing is new under the sun). I also suspect that they are the ones behind pushing a race war between the "Whites" and the "Blacks." It is sort of a "divide and conquer" strategy. Not caring for either population of people, simply using each to accomplish an objective and self-serving end—World Rule. Yet, God said of the Children of Israel that they would *serve* their enemies in want of **all** things (i.e., in need of all things, lacking in all things). Whom does this better describe, the majority of Blacks scattered across the lands of this world or the European Jews?

Although Hebrew Israelites are judicially blinded currently, there *is* a great awakening unto their true heritage and identity forthcoming. Scripture deems it so.

[94]

*AND IT **SHALL** COME TO PASS, when all
these things are come upon thee, the blessing
and the curse, which I have set before thee,
and THOU **SHALL** CALL THEM TO MIND
among all the nations, whither the LORD thy
God hath driven thee, And SHALT RETURN
unto the LORD thy God, and SHALT OBEY his
voice according to all that I command thee this
day, thou and thy children, with all thine heart,
and with all thy soul; That **THEN** the LORD thy
God **will turn** thy captivity, and have
compassion upon thee, and **WILL RETURN
AND GATHER THEE** from all the nations,
whither the LORD thy God hath scattered thee.*
(Duet.30:1-3; emphasis added)

Thus, according to scripture, it is not a matter of
if but a matter of *when* the great awakening will
occur. Also according to scripture, this great
awakening will be followed by repentance and a
return unto God and His ways on the part of
Hebrew Israelites worldwide. There will also be a
"cleansing" and a gathering of them into their own
land at the Messiah's Return, *"And so all Israel
shall be saved: as it is written, There shall come out
of Sion the Deliverer, and shall turn away
ungodliness from Jacob: for this is my covenant
unto them, when I shall take away their sins"* (Rom.
11:26–27). These scriptures, and others reviewed
earlier, reveal that the future and final restoration of
Israel in the last days is not only a possibility but is
a fact—as it is a fact that God will also bring full
retribution to the nations and enemies of His
Chosen ones when Christ returns.

[95]

...though I make a full end of all nations whither I have scattered thee, yet I will not make a full end of thee... Therefore all they that devour thee shall be devoured; and all thine adversaries, every one of them, shall go into captivity; and they that spoil thee shall be a spoil, and all that prey upon thee will I give for a prey. (Jer. 30:11; 16; emphasis added)

...and I will punish all that oppress them. And their nobles shall be of themselves, and their governor shall proceed from the midst of them. (Jer. 30:20-21; emphasis added)

... for I will contend with him that contendeth with thee... And I will feed them that oppress thee with their own flesh.... (Isa. 49: 25-26)

For the nation and kingdom that will not serve thee shall perish; yea, those nations shall be utterly wasted... The sons also of them that afflicted thee shall come bending unto thee; and all they that despised thee shall bow themselves down at the soles of thy feet;... (Isa. 60: 12, 14; emphasis added)

Again, it is not a question of IF but WHEN a Great Awakening will occur among the now lost and judicially blinded Hebrew Israelites. I for one would rather that it be much sooner than later, given the great reward that awaits such an awakening and collective repentance.

Chapter Two:
A Rude Awakening

No one religion has a corner on absolute truth. Not even my own faith, the one to which I ascribe—Christianity. That is why I do not necessarily like titles or labels as such. I find that labels tend to bias one's perspective on how we see things. Depending on the label or title we are wearing (be it Christianity, Roman Catholicism, Mormonism, Jehovah Witness, Seventh-Day Adventist, Black Hebrew Israelite, etc.), we come to the table with preconceived notions and ideas of what is and is not truth, which prevents us from hearing and receiving The Truth. Much like the religious leaders in Jesus/Yehoshua's day, the scribes and the Pharisees spent so much time studying "truth," debating "truth," and claiming "truth" that they did not recognize Truth when HE came. Me, I do not want to be hindered by titles or labels. I am a seeker of Truth and *only* Truth. Therefore, I am determined to go wherever Truth takes or leads me, even if I have to make adjustments in my own way of thinking or my own way of living in order to line up with TRUTH.

In my search for truth, I am finding that almost every mainstream religion contains a mixture of truth and error, including Christianity. The proportion of truth and error may differ in varying degrees within each, but a mixture of truth and error exits nonetheless. The enemy has so cleverly strategized the religious system as such that it keeps us from even considering what truth another religion or faith may hold that our own lacks and what error exists in our own faith that we must cease to embrace. In this section, we will take another biblical journey through the scriptures in search of truth. In taking this journey, however, we must at times prepare ourselves for A Rude Awakening.

First of all, my hat goes off to the many Hebrew Israelites who have awakened and who continue to awaken other Hebrew Israelites to their true identity as bloodline descendants of the biblical Israelites—descendants of Hebrew Israelites who fell victim to the Transatlantic and Indian Ocean slave trades and who were scattered throughout the four corners of the world, as God forewarned. That they are descendants who now live in obscurity among the Gentiles in the lands they have been scattered to and are currently exiled in. This truth is so well supported by scriptural, archeological, historical, and scientific evidence that it is astounding. The author, however, beseeches each reader to pray and prayerfully research for him or herself and see if this truth be not so.

While credit, deservedly, is given to Hebrew Israelites camps for enlightening fellow Hebrew Israelites to the truth of their heritage and identity, it is nevertheless disheartening to hear some of them spew out hatred and automatically exclude a particular group of people from being recipients of

God's grace, mercy, and blessings of Salvation because they are not Hebrew Israelites or physical descendants of the Biblical Hebrew Israelites. They are globally cast as "heathens" and "doomed Edomites," as though the mere color of their skin or the fact that they are not physical/bloodline descendants of Abraham, Isaac, and Jacob alone will keep them out of the Kingdom of God. Well herein is the first rude awakening. The mere color of a person's skin or the fact that he or she is not a physical descendant of Abraham, Isaac, and Jacob is *not* the thing that is going to keep one out of the Kingdom of God. Just like the mere color of your skin and my skin or the fact that we may be bloodline descendants of Abraham, Isaac, and Jacob is not the thing that is going to *guarantee* our entrance INTO the kingdom of God.

This exclusion from the Kingdom of God based merely on one being a Gentile versus a physical or natural Israelite or Jew is not scriptural. Scripture tells us that God so loved the WORLD that He gave his only begotten son that WHOSOEVER believeth in him should Not perish, but have everlasting life (John 3:16). Scripture does not say, "For God so loved the Jews, or God so loved the Children or the Nation of Israel that he gave His only begotten son..." It says, that "God so loved the World that He gave His only begotten son" that *whosoever* (be it Jew, Gentile, male, female, young, old, rich, poor, Red, Yellow, Brown, Black or White) believeth in him should NOT perish but have Eternal Life.

A prototype of the eventual inclusion of both Gentiles and Jews into the Kingdom of God or His

[99]

household of faith can even be seen in the Old Testament Law. In the Law, God gives instructions to the Children of Israel on how they were to treat a "stranger" or a "foreigner." The terms "stranger" or "foreigner" are oftentimes used interchangeably in scripture and refer to a person who is a citizen of a different country. Thus, a foreigner/stranger in the Bible usually referred to someone who was foreign to the Hebrew People (Lockyer, 392). In other words, it was someone who was not a citizen of Israel and foreign to the covenant God made with Israel. However, look at the way God commanded the Children of Israel to treat the foreigners or strangers who lived among them.

> *He doth execute the judgment of the fatherless and widow, and <u>loveth the stranger, in giving him food and raiment. Love ye therefore the stranger</u>: for ye were strangers in the land of Egypt.* (Deut. 10:18-19; emphasis added)

> *Thus saith the LORD; <u>Execute ye judgment and righteousness</u>, and deliver the spoiled out of the hand of the oppressor: and do no wrong, <u>do no violence to the stranger,</u> the fatherless, nor the widow, neither shed innocent blood in this place.* (Jer. 22:3; emphasis added)

> *<u>Also thou shalt not oppress a stranger: for ye know the heart of a stranger</u>, seeing ye were strangers in the land of Egypt.* (Exod. 23:9; emphasis added)

> *Ye shall have **one manner of law,** <u>as well for the stranger, as for</u> <u>one of your own country:</u> for I am the LORD your God.* (Lev. 24:22; emphasis added)

[100]

Also note the prayer that Solomon prayed at the Temple Dedication.

Moreover concerning <u>a stranger</u>, that is not of thy people Israel, but <u>cometh out of a far country</u> for thy name's sake; (For they shall hear of thy great name, and of thy strong hand, and of thy stretched-out arm;) <u>when he shall come and pray</u> toward this house; <u>Hear thou in heaven</u> thy dwelling place, and <u>do according to <u>all that the stranger calleth to thee for</u>: that all people of the earth may know thy name, to fear thee, as do thy people Israel; and <u>that they may know that this house, which I have builded, is called by thy name.</u> (1King 8:41-43; emphasis added)

*<u>Also the sons of the stranger, that join themselves to the LORD, to serve him, and to love the name of the LORD, to be his servants,</u> **every one** <u>that keepeth the sabbath from polluting it, and taketh hold of my covenant; Even them will I bring to my holy mountain, and make them joyful in my house of prayer:</u> their burnt offerings and their sacrifices shall be accepted upon mine altar; <u>for mine house shall be called an house of prayer</u> for **all** people. (Isa. 56:6-7; emphasis added)*

*So shall ye divide this land unto you according to the tribes of Israel. And it shall come to pass, <u>that ye shall divide it by lot for an inheritance unto you, **and to the strangers** that sojourn among you,</u> which shall beget children among you: <u>and they shall be unto you as born in the country among the children of Israel; they shall have inheritance WITH you among the tribes of Israel. And it shall come to pass,</u>*

that in what tribe the stranger sojourneth,
there shall ye give him his inheritance, saith
the Lord GOD. (Ezek. 47:21-23; emphasis
added)

...Of the tribe of Zabulon were sealed twelve
thousand. Of the tribe of Joseph were sealed
twelve thousand. Of the tribe of Benjamin were
sealed twelve thousand. **After this,** *I beheld,*
and, lo, a great multitude, *which no man could*
number, *of all nations, and kindreds and*
people, and tongues, stood before the throne,
and before the Lamb, *clothed with white robes,*
and palms in their hands; And cried with a
loud voice, *saying, Salvation to our God* *which*
sitteth upon the throne, and unto the Lamb.
(Rev. 7:5-10; emphasis added)

Besides the aforementioned passage in
Revelation, below are additional New Testament
scriptures that also recognize *both* **redeemed** Jews
and Gentiles as being partakers in the Kingdom of
God.

That the Gentiles should be *fellowheirs,* *and of*
the same body, and *partakers* *of his promise in*
Christ by the gospel. (Eph. 3:6; emphasis
added)

Wherefore remember, that ye being in time
past Gentiles in the flesh, *who are called*
Uncircumcision by that which is called the
Circumcision in the flesh made by hands; *That*
at that time ye were without Christ, being
aliens from the **commonwealth of Israel,** *and*
strangers from the covenants of promise,
having no hope, and without God in the world:
But now in Christ Jesus *ye who sometimes*

*were far off are made nigh by the blood of Christ. For he is our peace, who hath made both one, and hath broken down the middle wall of partition between us.... Now therefore ye are no more strangers and foreigners, but fellow **citizens** with the saints, and of the household of God;* (Eph. 2:11-14, 19; emphasis added).

Thus, these scriptures demonstrate that God planned from the beginning to include both Gentile and Jews into His Kingdom or household of faith. Furthermore, although God's *everlasting* covenant was made with the Children of Israel, He did not by any means prohibit a non-Israelite or non-Jew from *sharing or partaking* of the *covenant blessings of Israel* who desired to partake of them *under the terms He so prescribed*, however (Isa 56:2-8). Non-Jews were welcomed into His Kingdom. Thus, the conversion of Cornelius and his friends and relatives (Act 10:1-45), the conversion of the Philippian jailer and his household (Acts 16:25-34), and the conversion of countless Gentiles under Paul's ministry (the Epistles of Paul). Also, let us not forget about Tamar, a Canaanite; Rahab, a Canaanite; and Ruth, the Moabite, who proclaimed to her mother-in-law Naomi *"...whither thou goest, I will go; and where thou lodgest, I will lodge: thy people shall be my people, and thy God my God:"* (Ruth 1:16). These were all non-Israelite women or non-Jews who became not only part of Israel but who also became part of the very lineage or genealogy of our Savior Jesus/Yehoshua—who was born a Jew after the flesh. How more acceptable in the family of God can you get?

[103]

Additionally, scripture tells us that the gospel of Christ *is the power of God unto Salvation to EVERYONE that believeth; to the Jew first and ALSO to the Greek* (Rom 1:16; emphasis added). The scripture does not say "to the Jew ONLY" but "*to the Jew first*". Thus, the opportunity for salvation would be given to the Jews first and then extended to the Gentiles until the *fullness of the Gentiles has come in*. The specific call of Paul into the Ministry by Christ Himself was for this very reason. Here is what Jesus/Yehoshua said unto Ananias concerning Paul ... "*Go your way: for he is a chosen vessel to me, to bear my name before the Gentiles, and kings, and the children of Israel*" (Act 9:15; emphasis added).

The earthly ministry of Jesus/Yehoshua itself reflected the principle of bringing salvation to the Jews first then to the rest of the world. At the beginning of His ministry and after choosing his twelve disciples, He sent them forth saying, "*Go not into the way of the Gentiles, and into any city of the Samaritans enter ye not. But go rather to the lost sheep of the house of Israel*" (Matt. 10:5-6; emphasis added). However, at the end of his earthly ministry He commanded them saying, "*Go ye into all the world, and preach the gospel to every creature*" (Mark 16:15; emphasis added). In Acts 1:8, He said unto them, "*But ye shall receive power, after that the Holy Ghost is come upon you: and ye shall be witnesses unto me both in Jerusalem, and in all Judaea, and in Samaria, and unto the uttermost part of the earth*" (emphasis added).

[104]

When Jesus/Yehoshua told the Samaritan woman at the well, "Salvation is of the Jews," He was not saying that salvation was *just for* the Jews. He was simply acknowledging that salvation *came out* from the Jews. That God used the Jews as His instrument through which to bring the message of salvation. Thus, salvation came out from the Jews or the Jewish Nation as the Messiah, Savior of the World, was born a Jew *after the flesh* (Pedrin). The Jews were to take the message of the Kingdom of God and God's salvation offered through His son, Jesus/Yehoshua, to the rest of the world. As Hebrew Israelites, our forefathers failed miserably in their responsibility to God. Instead of being and sharing the light to others, they rejected the light or hid it under a bushel. For this reason, God turned to "*another people*" that were "*not his people*" to carry out this task. "*And ye shall leave your name <u>for a curse</u> unto my chosen: for the Lord GOD shall slay thee, and <u>call his servants by **another** name:</u>*" (Isa. 65:15; emphasis added). God also said, "*This people have I formed for myself;* [meaning the Gentiles whom he would convert] *they shall shew forth my praise. <u>But thou</u> <u>hath not called on me, O</u> <u>Jacob;</u> but thou hast been weary of me, O Israel*" (Isa.43:21-23; emphasis added). He said also in Romans: "*...I will call **them** <u>my people, which were</u> <u>not my people, and her beloved, which was not</u> <u>beloved.</u> And it shall come to pass, that <u>in the place</u> <u>where it was said unto them, Ye are not my people;</u> <u>there shall they be called the children of the living</u> <u>God</u>*" (Rom. 9:25-26; emphasis added).

God further declared:

"For from the rising of the sun even unto the going down of the same my name shall be great among the Gentiles; and in every place incense shall be offered unto my name, and a pure offering: for my name shall be great among the heathen, saith the LORD of hosts. But ye [Israel] have profaned it, in that ye say, the table of the LORD is polluted; and the fruit thereof, even his meat, is contemptible. (Mal. 1:11-12; emphasis added)

Therefore, Israel, as a nation and a people, has been set aside (for now). Hebrew Israelites as God's Chosen people have been judicially blinded. "A blindness" to God, to His way and to our heritage, has come upon us as a people who repeatedly disobeyed God; and failed as a nation to embrace Christ/Yehoshua and His gospel: *He came unto his own, and his own received him not* (John 1:11). The Most High God intended His Chosen People Israel to be a light unto the Gentiles with the gospel. However due to our forefathers' disobedience and rejection of the Messiah and His message, God turned to the Gentiles for the task of sharing the gospel. This task, however, will revert to the Jews, his Chosen People in the last days (Isa. 2:1-3; Mic. 4:1-2; Zech. 8:20-23).

Many Hebrew Israelites today who are coming into the knowledge of who they are as true bloodline descendants of Abraham, Isaac, and Jacob seem to be making the same mistakes that our forefathers made, however. Our forefathers took a "pharisaical" attitude and extreme pride in the fact that they were children or sons of Abraham after the

[106]

flesh. This proud and haughty spirit led them to believe that they were invincible, above all others, and accountable to no one simply because they were natural Jews or "God's Chosen People." However, the same warning that John the Baptist gave to the Pharisees of his day still applies to Hebrew Israelites of today: *"And think not to say within yourselves, We have Abraham to our father: for I say unto you, that God is able of these stones to raise up children unto Abraham"* (Matt. 3:9). Romans further notes that one is not a Jew outwardly but rather inwardly:

> *And shall not uncircumcision, which is by nature, **if it fulfil the law,** <u>judge thee,</u> who by the letter and circumcision dost transgress the law? For he is not a Jew, which is one outwardly; neither is that circumcision, which is outward in the flesh: But he is a Jew, which is one inwardly; and <u>circumcision</u> is that of the heart, in the spirit, and not in the letter; whose praise is not of men, but of God.* (Rom. 2:27-29; emphasis added)

Jesus/Yehoshua himself proclaimed:

> *.... Verily, verily, I say unto thee, Except a man be <u>born again</u>, he cannot see the kingdom of God... Except a man <u>be born of water and of the Spirit</u>, he cannot enter into the kingdom of God, That which is born of the flesh is flesh; and that which is born of the Spirit is spirit. Marvel not that I said unto thee, Ye must be <u>born again</u>.* (John 3:3, 5-7; emphasis added)

[107]

Finally, entrance into His Kingdom is *not of him that willeth nor of him that runneth but of God that sheweth mercy* (Rom. 9:16).

I would caution, therefore, those of us who are coming into the knowledge of our true heritage as Hebrew Israelites *not* to make the same mistake as our forefathers who fell into a false sense of pride and invincibility simply because they were the physical seed or descendants of Abraham, Isaac, and Jacob. Merely being a physical descendant of Abraham, Isaac, and Jacob did not guarantee their entrance into the Kingdom. In fact it was pride in this very fact that made them haughty, unfit and unworthy of the Kingdom of God. Behold the words of Jesus/Yehoshua,

> *And Jesus saith unto him, I will come and heal him. The centurion answered and said, Lord, I am not worthy that thou shouldest come under my roof: but speak the word only, and my servant shall be healed. For I am a man under authority, having soldiers under me: and I say to this man, Go, and he goeth; and to another, Come, and he cometh; and to my servant, Do this, and he doeth it. When Jesus heard it, he marvelled, and said to them that followed,* **Verily** *I say unto you, I have not found so great faith, no, not in Israel. And I say unto you, That* **many** *shall come from the east and west, and shall sit down with Abraham, and Isaac, and Jacob, in the kingdom of heaven. But the children of the kingdom shall be cast out into outer darkness: there shall be weeping and gnashing of teeth.* (Matt. 8:7-12; emphasis added)

A word to the wise is sufficient. Additionally, it may be somewhat of a rude awakening that scripture also makes it clear that the promises God made to Abraham and his descendants were not through the Law but through the righteousness of faith.

> For the promise, that he should be the heir of the world, _was not to Abraham, or to his seed, through the law, but through the righteousness of faith. For if they which are of the law be heirs, faith is made void, and the promise made of none effect_: . . . _Therefore it is of faith, that it might be by grace; to the end the promise might be sure to all the seed_; not to that _only_ which is of the law, but to that _also_ which is of the faith of Abraham; who is the father of us all, (Rom. 4:13-16; emphasis added)

Thus, faith seems to take pre-eminence over the Law or at least levels the playing field, between the Jew and the Gentile and their right even to inherit the covenant promises of God.

To be sure, it is a grave error for Hebrew Israelites to cast off, globally, a group of people from the Kingdom of God simply because they are not Hebrew Israelites or merely on the bases of their skin color. However, it is equally a grave error to say that God has cast off Israel, His Chosen People, forever and has replaced them with the Church. Although Israel has been judicially blinded to their identity, heritage, and inheritance and has been set aside for now, this is not to say that God has cast off Israel forever or has replaced her with the Church.

[109]

God has NOT done away with His Chosen People, Israel, or replaced them with the Church. This replacement theology is one of the most erroneous doctrines that is being taught by various groups today. Replacement theology requires a spiritualization of the word "Israel" that is not entirely supported by scripture. This camp, and the like, argues that Israel is now composed of all those who believe in Jesus/Yehoshua as Messiah and is now called the Church. Thus, they argue that "The Church" today is now "True Israel." They further argue that the salvation gospel is now coming from "*Spiritual Jews*" called the Church. Their argument is based on Romans 2:28-29, cited earlier:

> *For he is not a Jew, which is one outwardly; neither is that circumcision, which is outward in the flesh: But he is a Jew, which is one inwardly; and circumcision is that of the heart, in the spirit, and not in the letter; whose praise is not of men, but of God.*

Using this same scripture, another train of thought is this: "… Followers of Christ have not *replaced* Israel… the followers of Christ *are* Israel—Spiritual Israel" (Davies[1]).

Scripture, it seems, supports neither of these positions. The Church, in scripture, is never called "Israel" or even "Spiritual Israel." Although "*the*

---

[1] This Davies quote was actually taken from a website presenting an article with the same title also written by Davies. However, at the author's request, only one specified website is noted in Works Cited.

[110]

elect of God according to foreknowledge of the Father" is referred to as a *"spiritual house"* (1 Peter 1:1-2; 2:5), Peter never calls the Church [or believers] "spiritual Israel" (Kelly[2]; emphasis added). And, too, while Peter calls believers in 1Peter 2:10 "now the *people* of God" he never calls them "the *Israel* of God."* According to Bible commentator William McDonald, the "Israel of God" refers to natural Jews by birth who accepted the Lord Jesus as Messiah, not the Church, as many take it to mean (1898). Moreover, while Abraham is the father of *all believers* by faith (Rom. 4:16), **believers** are called *the children* of Abraham (Gal. 3:7) or *Abraham's seed* (Gal. 3:29), "...believers are not called Israel; only believing Jews (Israelites) are called Israel" (Kelly). Also, Paul does not equate Gentile believers with Israel. When he uses the word "Israel" in Romans 9:1-5, he is referring to his kinsmen after the *flesh—not* to *Gentile believers.* Thus, as believers, we are *all children of God* by faith (Gal. 3:26), but we are *not all Israelites* (Kelly; emphasis added).

So, those who try to "spiritualize" the word *Israel* (by saying that "Israel" is now the Church or that Israel now consists of *all* saints who believe in and follow Christ) do not seem to be supported by

---

[2] All information obtained from an article entitled, "Unconditional Promises to Israel" written by Mr. Russell Kelly is being used with his permission. Please note, however that his article was written within a contextual position held by Mr. Kelly that the 1948 State of Israel was a fulfillment of biblical prophecy regarding the Jews.

scripture. However, for the sake of argument, let us concede for a moment that there may be a "spiritual" implication represented by the word "Israel" in scripture. This still does not negate or annul any of the *literal* promises that God has made to physical or ethnic Israel. God's word is often dichotomous or allegorical in nature. This means that the Word often has both a spiritual and a physical/natural significance at the same time. For example, the life story of Hagar and Sarah is allegorical in nature, illustrating two covenants—the covenant of grace (Sarah the freewoman) and the covenant of the Law (Hagar—the bondwoman). The slave children of the bondwoman, Hagar, represent unbelieving Jews who are still seeking to *obtain* righteousness through the keeping of the Law. The children of the freewoman, Sarah, are all believers who obtain justification by faith in Christ. Though the life-story of Hagar and Sarah is allegorical in nature and teaches a spiritual lesson, these women physically existed and God literally fulfilled the promise He made to each. For instance, God reaffirmed a promise to Hagar that He would make Ishmael a great nation (Gen. 21:17-18). God literally fulfilled that promise when from Ishmael came *twelve princes according to their nations* (Gen. 25:12-16). Even if one were to accept the notion that the word "Israel" has a spiritual implication, the same analogy described above can apply to ethnic Israel.

Thus, while the terms "Israel" or "God's Chosen People" may have implications for a "Spiritual Israel," consisting of "Spiritual Jews" or a redeemed

[112]

people in which there is *"neither Jew nor Greek,"* this, again, *does not* negate or annul the plans and promises that God has made and is yet to fulfill regarding physical or ethnic Israel; or, more specifically, to the redeemed among ethnic Israel. Just as God promised Hagar in the *natural world* to make Ishmael a great nation, which He literally fulfilled (even though she also personified a spiritual truth), God also will literally fulfill all the covenant promises that He has made to ethnic Israel. Rather than spiritualizing the words "Israel" or "God's Chosen People," scripture reveals a more accurate way to view the relationship between Israel—God's Chosen People—and converted Gentiles. In Romans 11:1-2, Paul asked the question, "Hath *God cast away his people?"* and then answers, *"God forbid. For I also am an Israelite, of the seed of Abraham, of the tribe of Benjamin. God hath not cast away his people, which he foreknew.* In verses 17-24 of this same chapter, Paul illustrates, using the olive tree, the relationship between redeemed Israel and converted Gentiles.

> *And if some of the branches be broken off, and* <u>*thou,*</u> ***being a wild olive tree***, *wert grafted in* ***among them***, *and* ***with them*** *PARTAKETH of* <u>*the root and fatness of the olive tree;*</u> *Boast not against the branches. But if thou boast, thou bearest not the root,* <u>*but the root thee.*</u> *Thou wilt say then, The branches were broken off, that I might be grafted in. Well; because* ***of*** ***unbelief*** *they were broken off, and thou standest* <u>*by faith.*</u> *Be not highminded, but fear: For if God* <u>*spared not*</u> ***the natural branches***,

take heed lest he also spare not thee. Behold
therefore the goodness and severity of God: on
them which fell, severity; but toward thee,
goodness, if thou continue in his goodness:
otherwise thou also shalt be cut off. And they
also, if they abide not still in unbelief, shall be
grafted in: for God is able to graft them in
again. For if thou wert cut out of the olive tree
which is wild by nature, and wert grafted
contrary to nature into a good olive tree: how
much more shall these, which be the natural
branches, be grafted into their own olive tree?
(Rom. 11:17-24; emphasis added)

Paul explains here, that the disobedient and unbelieving Jews who rejected Jesus/Yehoshua as the Messiah were themselves rejected and "broken off" from their own "olive tree," Israel. Paul showed that the *only way* to remain a *citizen of Israel* was to believe in Jesus/Yehoshua as Messiah. This *citizenship* was also offered to the Gentiles *on the same condition*. If they would put their faith in the Messiah of Israel, they would be made *fellow citizens* WITH Israel and thus become part of the household of God and partaker of the promises made to Abraham and his descendants (Davies; emphasis added).

These verses also illustrate how Old Testament scriptures, wherein God instructs Israel how to properly treat "foreigners" and "strangers" living among them, are reconciled with New Testament scriptures. Just as *strangers or foreigners* in the Old Testament who became *citizens* or a part of Israel, got to *share* in Israel's inheritance and covenant blessings according to the Law, all Gentiles that *become fellow citizens* of *redeemed* Israel will get to *share* in *Israel's end-time* inheritance and covenant blessings *according to the promise.* Thus, to say that God has cast off and has replaced the Nation or the Children of Israel with the Church is not scriptural.

God made an ***everlasting*** covenant with Abraham and his physical descendants through Isaac and Jacob. When God made His promise to Abraham, because he could swear by no greater, he swore by himself (Heb. 6:13). Thus, GOD WILL fulfill ALL the covenant promises He made to Abraham and his physical descendants. These promises will ultimately be fulfilled during the 1000-year reign, which is one of the primary purposes, if not *the* primary purpose for the millennial and literal rule of Christ on Earth. During this time, the Nation of Israel will be restored and vindicated before all her enemies. All strangers or converted Gentiles who *joined the citizenship* of *redeemed* Israel as believers by faith will also *partake or share in* Israel's end-time inheritance and covenant promises (Isa. 56:4-8; Ezek. 47:21-23; Rom. 4:13-16; Gal. 3:29).

The following scriptures reflect God's special relationship and *eternal* commitment to Israel.

> *And yet for all that, <u>when they be in the land of</u>*
> *<u>their enemies, I will not cast them away,</u>*
> *neither will I abhor them, to destroy them*
> *utterly, and to break my covenant with them:*
> *for I am the LORD their God. <u>But I will for their</u>*
> *<u>sakes remember the covenant of their</u>*
> *<u>ancestors, whom I brought forth out of the land</u>*

of Egypt in the sight of the heathen, that I might be their God: I am the LORD. (Lev. 26:44-45; emphasis added)

When the Most High divided to the nations their inheritance, when he separated the sons of Adam, he set the bounds of the people according to the number of the children of Israel. For the LORD's portion is his people; Jacob is the lot of his inheritance. (Deut. 32:8-9; emphasis added)

The counsel of the LORD standeth for ever, the thoughts of his heart to all generations. Blessed is the nation whose God is the LORD; and the people whom he hath chosen for his own inheritance. (Ps. 33:11-12; emphasis added)

Israel is called God's People forever:

For thou hast confirmed to thyself thy people Israel to be a people unto thee for ever; and thou, Lord, art become their God. (2 Sam. 7:24; emphasis added)

For thy people Israel didst thou make thine own people for ever; and thou, LORD, becamest their God. (1 Chron.17:22; emphasis added)

Art not thou our God, who didst drive out the inhabitants of this land before thy people Israel, and gavest it to the seed of Abraham thy friend for ever? (2 Chron. 20:7; emphasis added)

Thou shall no more be termed Forsaken [i.e. called Lo-ammi]*; neither shall your land any more be termed Desolate: but you shall be*

[116]

called Hephzibah [my delight is in her], *and your land Beulah* [married]*: for the LORD delights in you, and your land shall be married.* (Isa. 62:4)

Sing, O heavens; and be joyful, O earth; and break forth into singing, O mountains: for the LORD hath comforted <u>his people</u>, and will have mercy upon his afflicted. But <u>Zion</u> said, The LORD hath forsaken me, and my Lord hath forgotten me. Can a woman forget her sucking child, that she should not have compassion on the son of her womb? yea, they may forget, <u>yet will I not forget thee</u>. Behold, <u>I</u> <u>have graven thee upon the palms of my hands; thy walls are continually before me.</u> (Isa. 49:13-16; emphasis added)

As the mountains are round about Jerusalem, <u>so the LORD is round about his</u> <u>people</u> from henceforth even for ever. (Ps. 125:2; emphasis added)

Again, every promise that God has made to Abraham, Isaac, Jacob, and their descendants will literally be fulfilled, and they will be fulfilled during the Millennial Reign when Christ establishes His kingdom on Earth. During the Millennium, Israelites or Hebrew Israelites will literally be regathered by God from the four corners of the Earth, from all nations where **HE** hath scattered them (Deut. 30: 1-3; Isa. 11:11-12; Isa. 27:12; Jer. 23:7-8; Jer. 31:10-11; Ezek. 11:17; Ezek. 39:25-28; Ezek. 37:21-22). Hebrew Israelites will be bought back and restored to their promise land, Israel (Jer. 30:1-3, 8-11, 17-24; Ezek. 36:28; Ezek. 37:21-22, 25; Ezek. 39:21-29; Zeph. 3:19-20). The Davidic

[117]

Covenant will literally be fulfilled in which God promised David that his house and kingdom will be established forever (Jer. 23:5; Jer. 30:9; Jer. 33:15-17; Ezek. 34:23-24; Ezek. 37:24-25; Hos. 3:5; Luke 1:32-33). God will vindicate Israel and bring full retribution and punishment to her enemies (Jer. 30:8, 11, 16, 20; Zeph. 3:19-20; Isa. 49: 22-25; Isa.60:10, 12, 14-15; Isa. 61:3-7; Isa.54:3; Rev. 13:10). Jerusalem will be the center for worship with a physical temple *built by the Lord himself* and where priestly duties will *apparently* be reinstituted (Zech. 6:12-13; Zech. 14:16-18; Mic. 4:2; Isa. 2:3; Isa. 56:6-8; Ezek. 43:18-46:24), and Israel shall live in peace, and enjoy prosperity and the labor of their own hands (Jer. 30:10, 18-19; Jer. 31: 2-21; Isa. 65:17-25; Amos 9:13-15; Isa. 11:6-9).

Additionally, tables will be turned on Israel's enemies.

> *For the LORD will have mercy on Jacob, and will yet choose Israel, and set them in their own land: and the strangers shall be joined with them, and they shall cleave to the house of Jacob. And the people shall take them and bring them, to their place: and the house of Israel shall possess them in the land of the LORD for servants and handmaids: and they shall take them captives, whose captives they were; and they shall rule over their oppressors.* (Isa. 14:1-2; emphasis added)
>
> .... *Therefore all they that devour thee shall be devoured; and all thine adversaries, every one of them, shall go into captivity; and they that spoil thee shall be a spoil, and all that prey*

upon thee will I give for a prey. (Jer. 30:16; emphasis added)

And I will feed them that oppress thee with their own flesh; and they shall be drunken with their own blood, as with sweet wine: and all flesh shall know that I the Lord am thy Saviour and thy redeemer, the mighty One of Jacob. (Isa. 49: 26)

If any man have an ear, let him hear. He that leadeth into captivity shall go into captivity... (Rev. 13: 9-10)

As an aside, it appears that the Mormons had the right concept regarding a people being in servitude to another during the millennial and/or the eternal state. They just had the wrong people in servitude under the other (Isa. 14:1-2; Isa. 54:3).

All Israel will be saved.

And so all Israel shall be saved: as it is written, There shall come out of Sion the Deliverer, and shall turn away ungodliness from Jacob. For this is my covenant unto them, when I shall take away their sins. (Rom. 11:26-27; emphasis added)

And I will cleanse them from all their iniquity, whereby they have sinned against me; and I will pardon all their iniquities, whereby they have sinned, and whereby they have transgressed against me. (Jer. 33:8; emphasis added)

For I will take you from among the heathen, and gather you out of all countries, and will bring you into your own land. Then will I sprinkle clean water upon you, and ye shall be

[119]

clean: from all your filthiness, and from all your idols, will I cleanse you... Thus saith the Lord God; In the day that I shall have cleansed you from all your iniquities I will also cause you to dwell in the cities, and the wastes shall be builded. (Ezek. 36:24-25; 33; emphasis added)

The Salvation of the true natural Jews in the end-time can be likened unto the parable of the Prodigal Son found in Luke Chapter 15. God has always reserved for himself a remnant of faithful people *in each* generation. Thus, He has reserved for himself a redeemed remnant of Israel or Israelites today (Rom. 9:27-29). The rebellious member of the house of Jacob is the prodigal son and the faithful remnant of the house of Jacob is the older son. When the rebellious or prodigal son *came to himself,* and with *a repentant* heart *returned* home to his Father, the Father *RECEIVED* and *RESTORED* him to his *original* position of honor (i.e., grafted him back into his own olive tree) as **His son**. He said to his servants *"Bring forth the best robe, and put it on him; and put a ring on his hand, and shoes on his feet: And bring hither the fatted calf, and kill it; and let us eat, and be merry: For this my son was dead, and is alive again; he was lost, and is found. And they began to be merry.* The faithful son (or remnant) said unto his father, *"Lo, these many years do I serve thee, neither transgressed I at any time thy commandment: and yet thou never gravest me a kid, that I might make merry with my friends: But as soon as this thy son was come, which hath devoured thy living with harlots, thou hast killed for him the fatted calf"*. His father then said unto him, "*Son, thou art ever with me, and all that I have is thine. It was meet that we should make merry, and be glad: for this <u>thy brother was dead, and is alive again;</u> and was lost, and is found*" (Luke 15:23-32; emphasis added). Note now what Paul says in reference to Israel, "*Now if the fall of them be the riches of the world, and the diminishing of them the riches of the Gentiles; <u>how much more their fullness</u>... For if the casting away of them be the reconciling of the world, what shall the RECEIVING of them be, <u>but life from the dead</u>*" (Rom.11:15; emphasis added)?

Also, note the following scriptures regarding the salvation of Israel in the end-time.

> *Thy dead men shall live, together with my dead body shall they arise. Awake and sing, ye that dwell in dust: for thy dew is as the dew of herbs, and the earth shall cast the dead.* (Isa. 26:19)

> *And I will give them an heart to know me, that I am the LORD: and they shall be my people, and <u>I will be their God</u>: for they shall <u>return unto me</u> with their <u>whole heart.</u>* (Jer. 24:7; emphasis added)

> *And so <u>all Israel</u> shall be saved: as it is written, There shall come out of Sion the Deliverer, and shall turn away ungodliness from Jacob: <u>For this is my covenant unto them, when I shall take away their sins.</u> As concerning the gospel, they are enemies for your sakes: but as touching the election, they are beloved for the father's sakes. <u>For the gifts</u>*

and calling of God are without repentance.
(Rom11:26-29; emphasis added)

Here, it should be noted that *"all"* Israel is in reference to "believing" Israel as verse 23 of this same chapter denotes. *And they* [the Jews] *also, if they abide not still in unbelief, shall be grafted in: for God is able to graft them in again* (Rom.11:23; emphasis added). It should also be noted that scriptures, too, teach that a mass conversion of the Children of Israel world-wide will take place *after* they have been brought to a place of repentance. This mass salvation and/or cleansing of the Children of Israel in the end time will take place in like manner, as noted in Romans 11:26-27, Jerimiah 33:7-8; Ezekiel 36 :24-29,32-33 and Zechariah 13:1-2. However, note that God will also sift and test His people during the end-time great tribulation (also known as the day of Jacob's Trouble) where the only a small remnant will be found faithful *And I will bring the third part through the fire, and will refine them as silver is refined, and will try them as gold is tried: they shall **call on** my name, and I will hear them: I will say, It is my people: and they shall say, The LORD is my God* (Zech. 13:-9; emphasis added).

A New Covenant will also be made with the House of Israel and Judah:

> *Behold, the days come, saith the LORD, that I will make a new covenant with the house of Israel, and with the house of Judah, Not according to the covenant that I made with their fathers in the day that I took them by the hand to bring them out of the land of Egypt;*

[122]

which my covenant they brake, although I was an husband unto them, saith the LORD: But this shall be the covenant that I will make with the house of Israel; After those days, saith the LORD, I will put my law in their inward part , and write it in their hearts; and will be their God, and they shall be my people. And they shall teach no more every man his neighbour, and every man his brother, saying, Know the LORD: for they shall all know me, from the least of them unto the greatest of them, saith the LORD: for I will forgive their iniquity, and I will remember their sin no more. Thus saith the LORD, which giveth the sun for a light by day, and the ordinances of the moon and of the stars for a light by night, which divideth the sea when the waves thereof roar; The LORD of hosts is his name: If those ordinances depart from before me, saith the LORD, then the SEED of Israel also shall cease from being a nation before me for ever. (Jer. 31:31-36; emphasis added)

Israel's Spiritual and National Restoration in the Latter Days

The hand of the LORD was upon me, and carried me out in the spirit of the LORD, and set me down in the midst of the valley, which was full of bones, And caused me to pass by them round about: and, behold, there were very many in the open valley; and, lo, they were very dry. And he said unto me, Son of man, can these bones live? And I answered, O Lord GOD, thou knowest. Again he said unto me, Prophesy upon these bones, and say unto

[123]

them, O ye dry bones, hear the cause word of the LORD. Thus saith the Lord GOD unto these bones; Behold, I will cause breath to enter into you, and ye shall live:

...Then said he unto me, Prophesy unto the wind, prophesy, son of man, and say to the wind, Thus saith the Lord GOD; Come from the four winds breath, and breathe upon these slain, that they may live. So, I prophesied as he commanded me, and the breath came into them, _and they lived,_ and stood up upon their feet, an exceeding great army. Then he said unto me, Son of man, _these bones are the whole house of Israel:_ behold, they say, Our bones are dried, and our hope is lost: _we are cut off for our parts._ Therefore prophesy and say unto them, Thus saith the Lord GOD; _Behold, O my people, I will_ open your graves, and cause you to come up out of your graves, and bring you into the land of Israel And ye shall know that I am the LORD, when I have opened your graves, O my people, and brought you up out of your graves, And shall put my spirit in you, and ye shall live, and _I shall_ place you in your own land: then shall ye know that I the LORD have spoken it, and performed it, saith the LORD.

...Thus saith the Lord GOD; Behold, _I will_ take the children of Israel from among the heathen, whither they be gone, and will gather them on every side, and _bring them into their own land And I will make them one nation in the land upon the mountains of Israel; and one king shall be king to them all: and they shall be no more two nations,_ neither shall they be divided into two kingdoms any more at all: Neither

[124]

shall they defile themselves any more with their idols, nor with their detestable things, nor with any of their transgressions: but <u>I will</u> save them out of all their dwelling places, wherein they have sinned, <u>and will cleanse them</u>: so shall they be my people, and <u>I will</u> be their God. And David my servant shall be king over them; and they all shall have one shepherd: they shall also walk in my judgments, and observe my statutes, and do them.

*<u>And they shall dwell in the land that I have given unto Jacob my servant</u>, wherein your fathers have dwelt; and they shall dwell therein, <u>even they, and their children, and their children's children for ever</u>: **and my servant David shall be their prince for ever.*** (Ezek. 37 1-5, 9-14, 21-25; emphasis added)

Thus, God has NOT cast off His Chosen People forever. Nor has He replaced Israel with the "Church." Although as believers, (Israelite and Gentile alike) are one in the *Body* of Christ, (Gal. 3:28; Col. 3:9-11; 1 Cor.12:13), they nevertheless remain distinct groups within the people of God ("What does"). The Olive Tree prototype used by Paul illustrates this. Saved Gentiles that are grafted into the same olive tree are identified as "*wild branches*" that become *partakers* of the root and fatness of the olive tree. Redeemed Jews or Israelites, on the other hand, are called "*natural branches*" (Rom. 11:13-24). Additionally, Israel or more specifically the redeemed Israelites retain their rank of calling throughout eternity (Kelly; Rom. 1:16; Rom. 2:9-10; Isa. 60:10-12; Isa. 61:4-6; Rev. 7:2-10; Rev. 21:1, 10-14, 24; Ezek. 48:31-34).

[125]

Israel or the redeemed Children of Israel will also be restored to their original place of distinction and preeminence during the Millennium and/or eternal state (Isa. 60:10, 12, 14-15; Isa. 61: 5-6; Isa. 14:1-2; Isa. 49:23; Jer. 33:15-16; Zech. 8:23; Ezek. 45:8; 48:30-35).

In Acts 1:6-7 when the disciples came together, they asked Jesus, *"Lord, wilt thou at this time restore again the kingdom to Israel?"* (emphasis added). *And He said unto them, "It is not for you to know the times or the seasons, which the Father hath put in his own power."* Thus, the Jews in Jesus' day were expecting a promised restoration of the Kingdom to Israel. Therefore, following His resurrection, they wanted to know if Jesus/ Yehoshua would at that time restore the Kingdom to Israel. However, the promise of Israel's restoration to its place of preeminence among the nations will not be fulfilled until the last days.

Note, we often read this verse as if it says *"Lord, wilt thou at this time restore again the Kingdom OF Israel?"* However, the disciples asked, *"Lord, wilt thou at this time restore the Kingdom TO Israel?"* That is to say, Lord will you at this time restore the Glory of the Kingdom of God to Israel? Israel as a nation and a people at one point had the Glory or the presence of God with them. Note also that Jesus taught his disciples to pray to the Father, "THY KINGDOM COME"— not "ISRAEL'S" Kingdom Come. Thus, Israel will be restored to their place of preeminence in the last days because God will actually dwell in the midst of His people once again.

[126]

Sing and rejoice, O daughter of Zion: for, lo, I come, and I will dwell in the midst of thee, saith the Lord. (Zech. 2:10; emphasis added)

Moreover I will make a covenant of peace with them; it shall be an everlasting covenant with them: and I will place them, and multiply them, and will set my sanctuary in the midst of them for evermore. My tabernacle also shall be with them: yea, I will be their God, and they shall be my people. And the heathen shall know that I the LORD do sanctify Israel, when my sanctuary shall be in the midst of them for evermore. (Ezek. 37:26-28; emphasis added)

So, as scripture affirms, God has not forgotten his Chosen People nor has he replaced them with the "Church."

The tendency to spiritualize Israel and promote a replacement theology is not the only area of confusion. There also seems to be a great deal of confusion concerning where to place the Mosaic Law or Torah in the life of the Believer today. There is an apparent and earnest attempt on the part of Hebrew Israelites to return to keeping the Mosaic Law, including the dietary laws. Such an attempt is quite understandable. After all, was it not failure to keep all of God's laws, statutes, and commandments that caused Him to scatter the Hebrew Israelites throughout the nations where their descendants are currently experiencing the covenant curses of Deuteronomy 28 and Leviticus 26 in the *"land of their enemies"*? Thus, it just seems right to correct the mistake by returning to the keeping of the Law. Within the Christian Faith, there is confusion as to whether or not the Law should even be a part of the believer's life at all. To support their position, Christians typically point to the following scriptures:

> *For by grace are ye saved through faith; and that not of yourselves: it is the gift of God: Not of works, lest any man should boast.* (Eph. 2:8-9)

> *I do not frustrate the grace of God: for if righteousness come by the law, then Christ is dead in vain.* (Gal. 2:21)

> *O foolish Galatians, who hath bewitched you, that ye should not obey the truth, before whose eyes Jesus Christ hath been evidently set forth, crucified among you? This only would I learn of you, Received ye the Spirit by the works of the law, or by the hearing of faith? <u>Are ye so foolish? having begun in the Spirit, are ye now made perfect by the flesh?</u> Have ye suffered so many things in vain? if it be yet in vain. He therefore that ministereth to you the Spirit, and worketh miracles among you, doeth he it by the works of the law, or by the hearing of faith?* (Gal. 3:1-5; emphasis added)

> <u>*For as many as are of the works of the law are under the curse: for it is written, Cursed is every one that continueth not in all things which are written in the book of the law to do them. But that no man is **justified** by the law in the sight of God, it is evident: for, The just shall live by faith. And the law is not of faith:*</u> *but, The man that doeth them shall live in them. Christ hath redeemed us from the curse of the law, being made a curse for us: for it is*

[128]

written, Cursed is every one that hangeth on a tree: (Gal. 3:10-13; emphasis added)

Wherefore the law was <u>our schoolmaster to bring us unto</u> Christ, <u>that we might be justified by faith</u>. But after that faith is come, we are no longer under a schoolmaster. (Gal. 3:24-25; emphasis added)

Stand fast therefore in the liberty wherewith Christ hath made us free, and be not entangled again with the yoke of bondage. Behold, I Paul say unto you, that if ye be circumcised, Christ shall profit you nothing. For I testify again to every man that is circumcised, that he is a debtor to do the whole law. <u>Christ is become of no effect unto you,</u> whosoever of you are <u>justified by the</u> law; ye are <u>fallen from grace</u>. (Gal. 5:1-4; emphasis added)

Tell me, ye that desire to be <u>under the law, do ye not hear the</u> law? For it is written, that Abraham had two sons, the one by a bondmaid, the other by a freewoman. But he who was of the bondwoman was born after the flesh; but he of the freewoman was by promise. Which things is an allegory: for these are the two covenants; the one from the mount Sinai, which gendereth to bondage, which is Agar. For this Agar is mount Sinai in Arabia, and answereth to Jerusalem which now is, and is in bondage with her children. But Jerusalem which is above is free, which is the mother of us all. (Gal. 4:21-26; emphasis added)

Whom God hath set forth to be a propitiation through faith in his blood, to declare his righteousness for the remission of sins that are past, through the forbearance of God; To

[129]

declare, I say, at this time his righteousness: that he might be just, and the justifier of him which believeth in Jesus. Where is boasting then? It is excluded. By what law? of works? Nay: but by the law of faith. Therefore we conclude that a man is justified by faith without the deeds of the law. Is he the God of the Jews only? is he not also of the Gentiles? Yes, of the Gentiles also: Seeing it is one God, which shall justify the circumcision by faith, and uncircumcision through faith. (Rom. 3:25-30)

What shall we say then that Abraham our father, as pertaining to the flesh, hath found? For if Abraham were justified by works, he hath whereof to glory; but not before God. For what saith the scripture? Abraham believed God, and it was counted unto him for righteousness. Now to him that worketh is the reward not reckoned of grace, but of debt. But to him that worketh not, but believeth on him that justifieth the ungodly, his faith is counted for righteousness. (Rom. 4 1:5)

For sin shall not have dominion over you: <u>for ye are not under the law, but under grace.</u> (Rom.6:14; emphasis added)

Know ye not, brethren, (for I speak to them that know the law), how that the law hath dominion over a man as long as he liveth? For the woman which hath an husband is bound by the law to her husband so long as he liveth; but if the husband be dead, she is loosed from the law of her husband. So then if, while her husband liveth, she be married to another man, she shall be called an adulteress: but if her husband be dead, she is free from that law; so that she is no adulteress, though she be married to another man. Wherefore, my brethren, ye also are become dead to the law by the body of Christ; that ye should be married to another, even to him who is raised from the dead, that we should bring forth fruit unto God. For when we were in the flesh, the motions of sins, which were by the law, did work in our members to bring forth fruit unto death. But now we are delivered from the law, that being dead wherein we were held; that we should serve in newness of spirit, and not in the oldness of the letter. (Rom. 7:1-6; emphasis added)

But if the ministration of death, written and engraven in stones, was glorious, so that the children of Israel could not stedfastly behold the face of Moses for the glory of his countenance; which glory was to be done away: How shall not the ministration of the spirit be rather glorious? For if the ministration of condemnation be glory, much more doth the ministration of righteousness exceed in glory. For even that which was made glorious had no glory in this respect, by reason of the glory that excelleth. For if that which is done away was glorious, much more that which remaineth is glorious. Seeing then that we have such hope, we use great plainness of speech: And not as Moses, which put a veil over his face, that the children of Israel could not stedfastly look to the end of that which is abolished: But their minds were blinded: for until this day remaineth the same vail untaken away in the reading of the old testament;

[131]

*which vail is done away in Christ. But even
unto this day, when Moses is read, the vail is
upon their heart. Nevertheless when it shall
turn to the Lord, the vail shall be taken away.*
Now the Lord is that Spirit: and where the
Spirit of the Lord is, there is liberty. (2 Cor.
3:7-17; emphasis added)

However, how then are we to reconcile these
aforementioned verses with the following?

*Think not that I am come to destroy the law, or
the prophets: I am not come to destroy, but to
fulfil. For verily I say unto you, Till heaven and
earth pass, one jot or one tittle shall in no wise
pass from the law, till all be fulfilled.
Whosoever therefore shall break one of these
least commandments, and shall teach men so,
he shall be called the least in the kingdom of
heaven: but whosoever shall do and teach
them, the same shall be called great in the
kingdom of heaven.* (Matt. 5:17-19; emphasis
added)

*He that saith, I know him, and keepeth not his
commandments, is a liar, and the truth is not in
him.* (1 John 2:4; emphasis added)

If you love me, keep my commandments. (John
14:15; emphasis added)

*If you keep my commandments, you will abide
in my love, just as I have kept my Father's
commandments and abide in his love.* (John
15:10; emphasis added)

*And a certain ruler asked him, saying, Good
Master, what shall I do to inherit eternal life?
And Jesus said unto him, Why callest thou me*

good? none is good, save one, that is, God. Thou knowest the commandments, Do not commit adultery, Do not kill, Do not steal, Do not bear false witness, Honour thy father and thy mother. And he said, All these have I kept from my youth up. Now when Jesus heard these things, he said unto him, Yet lackest thou one thing: sell all that thou hast, and distribute unto the poor, and thou shalt have treasure in heaven: and come, follow me. And when he heard this, he was very sorrowful: for he was very rich. And when Jesus saw that he was very sorrowful, he said, How hardly shall they that have riches enter into the kingdom of God! For it is easier for a camel to go through a needle's eye, than for a rich man to enter into the kingdom of God. (Luke 18:18-25; emphasis added)

And it is easier for heaven and earth to pass, than one tittle of the law to fail. (Luke 16:17; emphasis added)

For not the hearers of the law are just before God, but the doers of the law shall be justified. For when the Gentiles, which have not the law, do by nature the things contained in the law, these, having not the law, are a law unto themselves: Which shew the work of the law written in their hearts, their conscience also bearing witness, and their thoughts the mean while accusing or else excusing one another.... (Rom. 2:13-15; emphasis added)

And the smoke of their torment ascendeth up for ever and ever: and they have no rest day nor night, who worship the beast and his image, and whosoever receiveth the mark of

[133]

*his name. Here is the patience of the saints: <u>here are they that keep the commandments of God,</u> **and** <u>the faith of Jesus.</u>* (Rev. 14:11-13; emphasis added)

So, how **do** we reconcile these verses of scriptures with the earlier ones? We reconcile them with the Word of God itself. It is amazing how God bridges the Old and the New Testaments teachings with His Word, bringing the two together with no contradiction whatsoever. Thus, the following scriptures can be used to reconcile these seemingly opposing scriptures:

Master, which is the great commandment in the law? Jesus said unto him, Thou shalt love the Lord thy God with all thy heart, and with all thy soul, and with all thy mind. This is the first and great commandment. And the second is like unto it. Thou shalt love thy neighbour as thyself. <u>On these two commandments hang all the law and the prophets.</u> (Matt. 22.36-40; emphasis added)

For <u>all</u> the law is fulfilled in one word, even in this; Thou shalt <u>love thy neighbour</u> <u>as thyself.</u> (Gal. 5:14; emphasis added)

For Christ is the end of the law <u>for righteouness</u> to everyone that believeth. (Rom.10:4; emphasis added)

Owe no man any thing, but to love one another: <u>for he that loveth another hath fulfilled the law.</u> For this, Thou shalt not commit adultery, Thou shalt not kill, Thou shalt not steal, Thou shalt not bear false witness, Thou shalt not covet; and if there be

[134]

any other commandment, it is briefly comprehended in this saying, namely, Thou shalt love thy neighbour as thyself. Love worketh no ill to his neighbour: therefore love is the fulfilling of the law. (Rom. 13:8-10; emphasis added)

Now the end of the commandment is charity [love] *out of a pure heart, and of a good conscience, and of faith unfeigned* [i.e., sincere faith]. (1 Tim.1:5; emphasis added)

And, behold, one came and said unto him, Good Master, what good thing shall I do, that I may have eternal life? And he said unto him, Why callest thou me good? there is none good but one, that is, God: but if thou wilt enter into life, keep the commandments. He saith unto him, Which? Jesus said, Thou shalt do no murder, Thou shalt not commit adultery, Thou shalt not steal, Thou shalt not bear false witness, Honour thy father and thy mother: and, Thou shalt love thy neighbour as thyself. The young man saith unto him, All these things have I kept from my youth up: what lack I yet? Jesus said unto him, If thou wilt be perfect, go and sell that thou hast, and give to the poor, and thou shalt have treasure in heaven: and come and follow me. But when the young man heard that saying, he went away sorrowful: for he had great possessions. Then said Jesus unto his disciples, Verily I say unto you, That a rich man shall hardly enter into the kingdom of heaven. (Matt. 19:16-23; emphasis added)

This last scripture in particular implies that, even if one were able to keep the letter of the Law *perfectly and entirely*, there is STILL something

[135]

that a person can lack which can keep him from making it into the Kingdom of God. What would *that* Lack be? The **lack** of the Law of LOVE in ACTION!

Consider the parable below:

When the Son of man shall come in his glory, and all the holy angels with him, then shall he sit upon the throne of his glory: And before him shall be gathered all nations:... And he shall set the sheep on his right hand, but the goats on the left. Then shall the King say unto them on his right hand, Come, ye blessed of my Father, inherit the <u>kingdom</u> prepared for you from the foundation of the world: For <u>You kept all of the commandments</u>. No, he said, For I was a hungred, and ye gave me meat: I was thirsty, and ye gave me drink: I was a stranger, and ye took me in: Naked, and ye clothed me: I was sick, and ye visited me: I was in prison, and ye came unto me. Then shall the righteous answer him, saying, Lord, when saw we thee a hungred, and fed thee? or thirsty, and gave thee drink? When saw we thee a stranger, and took thee in? or naked, and clothed thee? Or when saw we thee sick, or in prison, and came unto thee? And the King shall answer and say unto them, Verily I say unto you, Inasmuch as ye have done it unto one of the <u>least</u> of these my brethren, ye have done it unto me.

Then shall he say also unto them on the left hand, Depart from me, ye cursed, into everlasting fire, prepared for the devil and his angels: For I was a hungred, and ye gave me no meat: I was thirsty, and ye gave me no drink: I was a stranger, and ye took me not in:

*naked, and ye clothed me not: sick, and in
prison, and ye visited me not.... And these will
go away to everlasting punishment, but the
righteous into eternal life.* (Matt. 25:31-46)

The difference between the two groups is Love
in action. Thus Love *is* the fulfillment of the Law
(Rom. 13:10). Love is the Righteousness of the
Law. The Law of love did not just appear in the
New Testament. It was ALWAYS a part of the Law
plainly stated at times ((Deut. 6:5; Lev. 19:17) and
explicitly implied at other times. Like in the
practical way God instructed the Hebrew Israelites
to treat one another and the strangers that lived
among them (see Lev. 19:9-18; Deut. 15:5-11;
Deut. 10:18-19; Jer. 22:3; Exod. 23:9). The Law of
Love is also explicitly implied in the Ten
Commandments. The first four Commandments
instructs us how to Love God (Exod. 20:3-11). The
last six Commandments instructs us how to love our
neighbor (Exod. 20:12-17). Thus, the Law shows us
practically how to love God and our neighbor.
When we walk in the law of Love, we fulfill the Law.
Consider the following scripture that demonstrates
this point.

*And, behold, a certain lawyer stood up, and
tempted him, saying, Master, what shall I do to
inherit eternal life? He said unto him, <u>What is
written **in** the law? HOW readest thou?</u> And he
answering said, Thou shalt love the Lord thy
God with all thy heart, and with all thy soul,
and with all thy strength, and with thy entire
mind; and thy neighbour as thyself. And he
said unto him, <u>Thou hast answered right: this</u>*

do, and thou shalt live. (Luke 10:25-28; emphasis added)

What in essence is written **in** the Law and what essentially the Law is all about is Love—love for God and love for our fellow man or neighbor wherein the lawyer aptly responded to the question when asked, *"What is written in the law? How readest thou?* Therefore, when we walk in the Law of Love we fulfill the Law of God because the Law of Love is what the Law of God is All About. We can never obtain righteousness or justification with God through the keeping of the letter of the Law. Justification comes only through Faith in Christ or Yehoshua. Once we are justified by faith, we then choose to live or walk according to His Holy and Righteous Standard, which is the Law or more specifically the Law of Love. The Law of Love is the Spirit and the Character of God and Christ or Yehoshua. When we walk according to another or according to our own righteous standard, then we are guilty of idolatry. We are guilty of violating the Law. We are guilty of violating the Law of Love. We are even guilty of violating the very Character of God—all of which is sin, for sin is the transgression of the Law. Only when we walk according to God's Righteous Standard, which in essence is walking according to the Law of Love, are we allowing Him to be Lord of our life.

Strangely enough, my growing love for the Father leads me not to reject or despise His commandments but to embrace them all the more— not for the sake of obtaining justification or to be found justified in his sight but because of the love

[138]

that I have for Him. Thus, I follow after the Law of Righteousness or rather the Law of Love, but I do so by faith and through God's grace that has been afforded me through the redemptive work of Christ, knowing that when I walk in the Law of Love I fulfill the Law of God.

As stated earlier, it seems as if Hebrew Israelites are attempting to please or find favor with God by returning to the Torah or by keeping the letter of the Law. This, again, seems like the right thing to do, since failure to do so is the reason why Hebrew Israelites are in their present-day captivity experiencing the covenant curses. Scripture has shown us, however, that *there is a difference* between keeping the letter of the Law in order to find *justification* or right-standing with God *versus* accepting justification through faith in Christ, then walking according to His way of righteousness or according to the Law of Love—knowing that Love is the fulfillment of the Law. One fosters legalism and pride in works of the flesh. The other fosters humility in the work of Grace. The verses below further illustrate the thin line between the two.

> *What shall we say then? That the Gentiles, which followed not after righteousness, have attained to righteousness, even the righteousness which is of faith. But Israel, which followed after the law of righteousness, hath not attained to the law of righteousness. Wherefore? Because they sought it not by faith, but as it were by the WORKS of the law. For they stumbled at that stumblingstone; As it is written, Behold, I lay in Sion a*

[139]

stumblingstone and rock of offence: and whosoever believeth on him shall not be ashamed. (Rom. 9:30-33; emphasis added)

Stand fast therefore in the liberty wherewith Christ hath made us free, and be not entangled again with the yoke of bondage. Behold, I Paul say unto you, that if ye be circumcised, Christ shall profit you nothing. For I testify again to every man that is circumcised, that he is a debtor to do the whole law. Christ is become of no effect unto you, whosoever of you <u>are justified</u> [i.e. seek justification] *by the law; <u>ye are fallen from grace.</u>* (Gal. 5:1-4; emphasis added)

Many Hebrew Israelites condemn Christians who believe they're justified by faith. The Hebrew Israelites seem to feel that the Christians' constant "we are no longer under the law but under grace" argument is an excuse to justify a not-so-disciplined life-style. Therefore, they condemn Christians for not following the Torah or Mosaic Law, including its dietary laws. I wonder, however if such strict adherence to the letter of the Law may actually be putting one in the apostate position of having *"fallen from grace." Especially* if the keeping of the Law is an attempt by one to seek justification or right standing with God, which we know can only be obtained through belief and faith in the redemptive work of Christ or Yehoshua. If such is the case, then the following scripture may be coming to pass right before our very eyes. *Let no man deceive you by any means: for that day shall not come, except there come a <u>falling away first,</u>* [from faith in Christ or Yehoshua] (2 Thess.

[140]

2:3; emphasis added). Thus scripture conveys that *works* of the Law *in the absence or in the place of grace or Faith in Christ or Yehoshua* lead to a state of apostasy or a great falling away from the faith. This is prophesied to take place in the end-time, prior to His return.

Pointedly on a similar note, I have heard Hebrew Israelites zealously condemn people to Hell for eating pork. Though I have come to believe that pork is not only unclean (physically) but unhealthy to the body, and for these reasons have recently stopped eating it, I am reminded of the following scripture below. While this passage of scripture may not necessarily pertain to clean and unclean meats as described in the Law, but to meats that have been offered up to idols, it still makes an important point about judging others:

> *For one believeth that he may eat all things: another, who is weak eateth herbs. Let not him that eateth despise him that eateth not; and let not him which eateth not judge him that eateth: for God hath received him. Who art thou that judgest another man's servant? to his own master he standeth or falleth. Yea, he shall be holden up: for God is able to make him stand.*
>
> *But why dost thou judge thy brother? or why dost thou set at nought thy brother? for we shall all stand before the judgment seat of Christ. For it is written, As I live, saith, the Lord, every knee shall bow to me, and every tongue shall confess to God. So then every one of us shall give account of himself to God. Let us not therefore judge one another any more: but judge this rather, that no man put a*

stumblingblock or an occasion to fall in his brother's way. I know, and am persuaded by the Lord Jesus, that there is nothing unclean of itself: but to him that esteemeth any thing to be unclean, to him it is unclean. But if thy brother be grieved with thy meat, <u>now walkest thou not charitably. Destroy not him with thy meat, for whom Christ died.</u> Let <u>not</u> then your good be evil spoken of: <u>For the kingdom of God is not meat and drink; but righteousness, and peace, and joy in the Holy Ghost.</u> For he that in these things serveth Christ is acceptable to God, and approved of men. Let us therefore follow after the things which make for peace, and things wherewith one may edify another. <u>For meat destroy not the work of God.</u> All things indeed are pure; but it is evil for that man who eateth with offence. It is good neither to eat flesh, nor to drink wine, nor any thing whereby thy brother stumbleth or is offended, or is made weak. Hast thou faith? have it to thyself before God. Happy is he that condemneth not himself in that thing which he alloweth And he that doubteth is damned if he eat, because he eateth not of faith: for whatsoever is not of faith is sin. (Rom.14:2-23; emphasis added)

This scripture reminds us to owe no man anything but to love him and leave the judging to God. *Who art thou that judgest another man's servant? to his own master he standeth or falleth. Yea, he shall be holden up: for God is able to make him stand* (Rom. 14:4). The scripture in James 4:11-12 also reminds us to *"Speak not evil one of another, brethren. He that speaketh evil of his brother, and judgeth his brother, speaketh evil of*

[142]

the law, and judgeth the law: but if thou judge the law, thou art not a doer of the law, but a judge. There is one lawgiver who is able to save and to destroy: who art thou that judgest another?"

I would now like to share excerpts from an article that I feel illustrates quite well the relationship between the Law and the Believer today. The article points out that there are two distinct laws—the Moral Law or the Decalogue, also known as the Ten Commandments, and The Book of the Law or the Law of Moses, containing laws, ordinances (i.e., ceremonial and/or sacrificial laws) and statutes or judgments. The Ten Commandments were written on two tablets, *by the finger of God*, and placed *inside* the arch (Deut. 10:1-5). The *Book of the Law* was written by Moses, as given to him by God, and placed on the SIDE of the arch (Deut. 31:24-26). Here is the excerpt from that article.

> God's Word speaks of two great laws. Law number 1 is the Law of God (the Ten Commandments, or Two tablets of the Testimony), also known as the moral law and the Decalogue. Law number 2 is the Law of Moses (the "Book of the Law," or "Book of the Covenant"), also known as the Mosaic Law, the Ordinances and the Ceremonial Law. Is there a relationship between these two laws? Absolutely. If an Israelite sinned, he broke law number 1, the moral law being the Ten Commandments. He then had to bring his offering according to law number 2, the sacrificial law to receive forgiveness. This is the relationship between these two laws. Law

[143]

number 1 defines sin, as sin is the transgression of the moral law, the Ten Commandments (1 John 3:4). Law number 2 defined sacrifices which was the remedy for sin.

If the Israelite sinned, he broke the first law. To make atonement for his sin he had to obey the second law. As can be clearly seen, here are two very distinct laws of which this fact is unmistakable. Jesus Christ permanently took the place of law number 2 when He cried out "It is finished" and bowed His head and died. When the unseen hand tore the temple curtain from top to bottom (Matthew 27:51), this signified that this sacrificial law system was once and for all time nailed to the cross.

. . . The perfect sacrifice of Jesus ended this whole sacrificial system once and for all, thankfully giving us no requirement to obey this law of bondage which pointed forward to the true sacrifice that saves us from our sins, which is transgression of the moral law, the Ten Commandments. When we sin now, we genuinely repent, confess our sin and through God's grace and faith in the sacrifice of Christ, we are forgiven. ("The Ceremonial Law")

Paul, in Romans 3:31, asks an excellent question, *"Do we then make void the law through faith? God forbid: yea, we establish the law"* (emphasis added) His answer is even more awesome. Here Paul lets us know again that there is no contradiction in acknowledging or keeping the (moral) Law of God and having faith in Christ. The latter (having faith in Christ) confirms the first (the

Law of God). Think about it. The first thing we do in order to be saved is to acknowledge that we are sinners and are in need of a savior. We then ask Christ/Yehoshua to come into our lives and save us from our sins. However, *without the Law* there can be no sin, since sin is the transgression of God's Law. Without sin (in the world), there would be no need for or faith in Christ (a Savior from sin). Thus, through our trust and faith in Christ to save us from our sins (which is the transgression of the Law) we verify, confirm, establish the validity and existence of the Law.

As mentioned at the beginning of the chapter, I do not particularly like titles as they tend to bias one's view or perspective on how one sees things, which oftentimes prevents us from hearing and receiving Real Truth. Again, I am a seeker of Truth, and I am determined to go wherever Truth takes or leads me, even if I have to make adjustments in my way of thinking or living in order to line up with TRUTH. Having said this let me ask this question: Where in *the Word of God* do we read where **God** changed His Sabbath day from the seventh day of the week to the first day of the week?

Even as a child, it boggled my mind why we were worshiping God on Sunday rather than on the seventh day, which is Saturday. When, at the age of seven, I realized that Sunday was the *first* day of the week and *not* the seventh, I exclaimed to my mother "We are worshipping on the *Wrong Day!*" She then proceeded to reassure me that Sunday Worship was okay because we were "Christians and not Jews." She continued to explain, "Sunday is our Sabbath day because Jesus rose from the dead on the first day of the week. Saturday is the Sabbath day for Jews because God gave that day to them." Over the years I was taught additional "justifications" for the Christian's "Sunday Sabbath" versus the seventh day Saturday Sabbath. However, I wonder how many ever stop to analyze and see the hypocrisy in some of these arguments while we trample a foot the Sabbath of the Lord?

Christians typically give the following rationales for keeping the "Sunday Sabbath." First, Sunday is the *Christian's* Sabbath because Jesus rose from the dead on the first day of the week (Matt. 28:1; Mark 16:1-2; Luke 24:1; John 20:1). Second, Pentecost or the birth of the "Church" took place on the first day of the week. Third, Paul told believers *"upon the first day of the week let every one of you lay by him in store, as God hath prospered him, that there be no gatherings when I come"* (I Cor. 16: 1-2). However, none of these reasons is a valid justification for annulling or changing the Day *that God Himself* established and decreed for HIMSELF since the beginning of creation. *"And on the seventh day God ended his work which he had made; and he rested on the seventh day from all his work which he had made. And **God** blessed the seventh day, and **sanctified** it: because that in it he had rested from all his work which God created and made"* (Gen.2:2-3). In Exodus 20:8-11 God said,

> *"Remember the sabbath day, to keep it holy. Six days shalt thou labour, and do all thy work: But the seventh day is the sabbath of the*

LORD thy God: in it thou shalt not do any work, thou, nor thy son, nor thy daughter, thy manservant, nor thy maidservant, nor thy cattle, nor thy stranger that is within thy gates. For in six days the LORD made heaven and earth, the sea, and all that in them is, and rested the seventh day: wherefore the LORD blessed the sabbath day, and hallowed it."

Regarding the rational offered by Christians using 1 Corinthian 16:1-2 to justify a "Sunday Sabbath," please note that the Sabbath was a day of rest and for a holy assembly or convocation unto God (Lev. 23:3). It was not a day for collecting money or items. This would have been a violation of the Sabbath and hence is why Paul had the believers collect money/items on the first day of the week so that no money/items would need to be collected *when he came*. Additionally, the scripture does not say that these believers were instructed to do this *"every"* first day of the week. The instruction Paul gave to these believers appears to have been for *that* particular visit. Even if one persists in misinterpreting the scripture to read as such, it still does not imply that Paul routinely met with believers for *Sabbath worship* on the first day of the week. Scripture tells us that it was *Paul's custom* to go into the synagogue and expound upon scripture on the Sabbath Day (Acts 17:2; 18:4), just as it was Jesus'/Yehosuah's custom (Luke 4:16). Be reminded, too, that it was *Paul* who said *to follow him as he followed Christ* (1 Cor. 11:1).

Another argument given by Christians for a Sunday Sabbath is "we are no longer under the law

[147]

but under grace". If this is the argument, then why turn around and honor Sunday as "the Sabbath day" and attribute to *it* all that should be attributed to God's Sabbath and claim that the reason for doing so is because, "God told us to 'Remember *the Sabbath day* and keep it holy'"? Do we not see that such reasoning is irrational and hypocritical? Besides, saying that we are no longer under the Law but under grace does not mean that the Law no longer has a place in our lives. It means that we are no longer under the *demands* of the Law that requires perfect obedience to it in order to be righteous or face the penalty of death because we are now under grace, which enables us to keep the Law and gives the remedy of forgiveness through the blood of Jesus/Yehoshua if we do not. Also, do we stop to consider the fact that Jesus/Yehoshua himself (whom we say is our example) kept the Sabbath while He was on Earth (Luke 4:16)? He even honored it in His death as He rested in the grave during the Sabbath then rose on the first day (Matt. 28:1, Mark 16: 1-2, Luke 24:1, John 20:1). Do we also stop to consider that every scripture that mentions Jesus/Yehoshua teaching in the Synagogue, says He did so on the Saturday Sabbath? When He was accused of breaking the Sabbath, it was on the seventh-day Sabbath, not Sunday.

After Christ's ascension into heaven the disciples and early believers, Gentiles and Jews alike, continued to honor the seventh-day Sabbath (Acts 17:1-2; Acts 13:13-15, 42-44; Acts 16:11-13; Acts 18:1-4). They continued to do so for the next two hundred years or up until the early to mid-AD 300s ("Sabbat"). Sunday in scripture is always referred to as the "first day of the week," never the Sabbath. However, the seventh day (Saturday) is always referred to as the Sabbath.

Another argument given for Sunday Sabbath-keeping is, **Paul** tells us that "One man esteemeth one day above another: another esteemeth every day alike. *Let every man be fully persuaded in his own mind.* He that regardeth the day, regardeth it unto the Lord; and he that regardeth not the day, to the Lord he doth not regard it" (Rom. 14:5-6). While this particular scripture may or may not be in reference to the Seventh Day Sabbath, let's concede that it is. So, if one desires to continue to esteem Sunday above any other day in regards to the Lord, fine, but call it what it is and what the scripture calls it: "The First Day of the Week". It is NOT the Lord's Sabbath. It is also not the "Christian Sabbath." *Scripturally, there is no such thing.*

Paul tells us also to *"Let no man therefore judge you in meat, or in drink, or in respect of a holyday, or of the new moon, or of the **sabbath days**"* (Col. 2:16; emphasis added). However, the sabbath *days* he is referring to in this verse are the *yearly* feast sabbath *days* of the Mosaic Law (Lev. 23:24-25, 27-32, 39-44) not the weekly Seventh **day** Sabbath of the Lord.

> *Remember the **sabbath day**, to keep it holy. **Six days** shalt thou labour, and do all thy work: But the **seventh day** is the **sabbath of the LORD thy God**: **in it** thou shalt not do any work, thou, nor thy son, nor thy daughter, thy manservant,*

nor thy maidservant, nor thy cattle, nor thy
stranger that is within thy gates...: wherefore
*the **LORD blessed** the **sabbath day, and**
hallowed it.* (Exod. 20:8-11; emphasis added)

One other argument given for Sunday Sabbath-keeping is that Saturday is the Sabbath day for the Jews, and Sunday is the Sabbath day for Christians. First of all, who decreed *two* different Sabbath days, one for Jews and one for Christians—God or man? As mentioned already, early believers, Jews and Gentiles alike, honored and worshipped on the Sabbath day of the Lord—the seventh day of the week, even hundreds of years following Christ's ascension. Additionally, although the Law was *only given to* the Jews that contained the Sabbath Day *command*, the laws were *not only for the Jews*. Strangers who lived among the Jews/Israelites and hoped to join themselves *with* them were *also* required to observe and do the laws as well (Exod. 12:48-49; Num. 15:29; Lev. 24:22). Thus, when Gentiles converted and became believers of the faith, they joined with believing Jews and continued to keep the Seventh day Sabbath of the Lord (Saturday). Note, especially, the word of God regarding the Sabbath in Isaiah 56:4-7.

For thus saith the Lord unto the eunuchs that
keep my sabbaths, and choose the things that
please me, and take hold of my covenant; Even
unto them will I give in mine house and within
my walls a place and a name better than of
sons and of daughters: I will give them an
everlasting name, that shall not be cut off. Also
the sons of the stranger, that join themselves to
the Lord, to serve him, and to love the name of

the Lord, to be his servants, EVERY ONE that
keepeth the sabbath from polluting it, and
taketh hold of my covenant; Even them will I
bring to my holy mountain, and make them
joyful in my house of prayer: their burnt
offerings and their sacrifices shall be accepted
upon mine altar; for mine house shall be
called an house of prayer for all people.
(Emphasis added)

To answer the question posed earlier, it was man, *NOT God,* who decreed or changed the Seventh Day Sabbath of the Lord to Sunday or the first day of the week. The Roman emperor Constantine enacted the first civil law regarding Sunday observance in AD 321 ("Sabbath"). He did this so that Christians and non-Christians would unite in observing the venerable day of the sun. Four years later, in AD 325, Pope Sylvester I officially named Sunday "the Lord's Day." In AD 338, Eusebius, the court bishop of Constantine, wrote, "All things whatsoever that it was the duty to do on the Sabbath (the seventh day of the week) we (Constantine, Eusebius, and other bishops) *have transferred* to the Lord's Day (the first day of the week) as more appropriately belonging to it" (qtd. in Thomsen). The change from Saturday to Sunday was later confirmed at a council of Bishops at the Council of Laodicea AD 363. In Daniel 7:25, God warned that a blasphemous power would seek to change times and laws, and the Catholic Church openly admits to doing it (Thomsen). For an in-depth study on this topic, see "Exactly Which Pope

Changed the Sabbath to Sunday?" by Michael Scheifler noted in the Suggested Resource section of book.

In the Peter Geiermann book, *Convert's Catechism of Catholic Doctrine*, we read:

Q. Which is the Sabbath day?

A. Saturday is the Sabbath day.

Q. Why do we observe Sunday instead of Saturday?

A. We observe Sunday instead of Saturday because the Catholic Church, in the Council of Laodicea [. . .] transferred the solemnity from Saturday to Sunday.

Q. Why did the Catholic Church substitute Sunday for Saturday?

A. The Church substituted Sunday for Saturday, because Christ rose from the dead on a Sunday, and the Holy Ghost descended upon the Apostles on a Sunday.

Q. By what authority did the Church substitute Sunday for Saturday?

A. The Church substituted Sunday for Saturday by the plenitude of that divine power which Jesus Christ bestowed upon her!

(Excerpt from *Convert's Catechism of Catholic Doctrine* by Peter Geiermann, C. SS. R. p. 50, TAN Books, Charlotte, NC www.tanbooks.com, used with permission).

In scripture we read that with God Almighty, "...*there is no variableness, neither shadow of turning*" (Jas. 1:17) and that He changes not ((Mal. 3:6). If God does not change, neither will His Law. "*My covenant I will not break, nor alter the thing that has gone out of My lips*" (Ps. 89:34; emphasis added). "*I know whatsoever God doth it shall be forever; nothing can be put* [added] *to it nor anything taken from it...*" (Eccles.3:14; emphasis added; Thomsen). Thus, there is no scriptural basis for changing or substituting the Lord's Seventh Day Sabbath to Sunday. What's more, God gave authority to no man to Change His Law.

As we see, scripturally there is no such thing as a *Jewish* Sabbath and a *Christian* Sabbath. It is the *Sabbath of the Lord* or *the Lord's Sabbath* which is the seventh day of the week that He commanded men to keep. Since coming into this knowledge, I continue to worship on Sundays, but I also observe the Sabbath from Friday evening to Saturday evening. However, should God lead me away from a Sunday worship entirely, I will not hesitate to obey. Every person must be led of the Holy Spirit regarding this and all things—especially Hebrew Israelites who are coming into the knowledge of their true heritage. As stated earlier, I am willing to go wherever truth leads me, even if it means making some necessary adjustments in my own life.

There was, yet, another adjustment I had to make four years ago as I stood in a Dollar Tree store searching for a particular ornament to hang on my Christmas tree. When I found the ornament, God impressed upon me that I should put it back

[153]

because that year would be the last time that I would put up a Christmas tree in my home. Not really understanding why that would be the case, I nevertheless put the ornament back and have not since put up a Christmas tree in my home. Christmas was my favorite time of the year. I got real joy in buying and giving gifts to family members and friends during Christmas. Although I continued to participate in these traditions of Christmas during those four years, I never put up a Christmas tree. The conviction was just too strong, and I knew it came from God. Within this past year, He gave me understanding and revelation as to why He had directed me in this manner. He opened up my understanding to the pagan origins of Christmas and its traditions, especially the Christmas tree.

Many Christians may not be aware that Christmas and its customs have their origins in pagan festivals that have nothing to do with Christ. That the customs in fact, *predate* the birth of Christ, existing thousands of years before Christ was born. They were customs related to mid-winter festivals ("Christmas"). These festivals were held to worship and celebrate the resurrection or rebirth of the SUN. They were held in various countries around the world in mid-winter when the days were shortest and the sunlight weakest. The people believed that, during this time, the sun god died and rose from the dead on December 25 as the newborn and venerable sun ("Origin"). During Saturnalia, a Roman mid-winter festival, the Romans decorated their homes and merriment filled the temples of ancient Rome, as sacred priests of Saturn, called dendrophori, carried wreaths of evergreen boughs in procession. These festivals were a time of merrymaking and exchanging of gifts ("Origin"). In Germany, they celebrated the Yule mid-winter festival, also in honor of the resurrected sun. Their celebration involved Yule singing, where people would go door to door, singing, and offering a drink in exchange for gifts ("Yule"). They believed that their various ceremonies gave the sun back its power.

All sun worship can ultimately be traced back to Babylon, an ancient city founded by Nimrod, the mighty hunter mentioned in Genesis. Scripture says that the beginning of his kingdom was Babel (Gen. 10:8-9). Legend has it that he married his own mother, Semiramis. When he died, his mother-wife, Semiramis, claimed a full-grown evergreen sprang overnight from a dead tree stump, symbolizing the bringing-forth of new life from the dead Nimrod (Collins). She also claimed that Nimrod's spirit had taken possession of the sun. She encouraged the people to pay homage to him by worshipping the sun-god. Therein began the evil practice of sun worship. When Semiramis later became pregnant, she claimed that she was miraculously overshadowed by her dead husband's spirit, the sun-god. In this way she was able to bring forth the son of the sun-god, whom she named Tammuz ("Who was").

Tammuz was born on December 25. Semiramis claimed that her son, Tammuz, was in actuality the returned or reborn Nimrod ("Who was"). Thus, the evergreen tree represented Nimrod resurrected as his own son Tammuz. On each anniversary of

[Tammuz]/Nimrod's birth, Semiramis claimed, Nimrod would visit the evergreen tree and leave gifts upon it (Collins). Since Tammuz was born on December 25, the day was highly honored and recognized by Nimrod's supporters. December 25 was therefore observed in honor of the birth of Tammuz long before Christianity existed and thousands of years before Christ was even born. Several centuries later, this pagan custom was "Christianized" as Christ's birthday, or Christmas ("Who was"). Think about it. December 25— known as the "nativity" of the **sun**, the date of ancient mid-winter pagan festivals and the birth date of every known sun-god (i.e., Tammuz/Horus, Mithra, Zeus, Amun-Ra)—was later determined to be the date **also** for the nativity of Christ. By the end of the fourth century, the whole of Christendom was celebrating Christmas (i.e., the "Mass of Christ," literally meaning the death of Christ) on December 25th. (For additional sources on the origin of Christmas, please see the Suggested Resource section).

A real eye-opener came for me this year as I was reading an article explaining why gifts are traditionally placed under a Christmas tree. The reason is that this placement requires a person to bend down to retrieve the gift from beneath the tree. Every time people kneel or bend down to retrieve a gift from beneath the Christmas tree, they are unwittingly kneeling or bowing down before a pagan idol symbolizing Nimrod. We find that many of our Christmas traditions are but variations of customs practiced by pagans many years ago. Thus, the syncretism of paganism and truth has crept into our lives, our traditions, and even in our worship that the Most High God clearly forbade and sternly warned against as abominable to Him.

Hear ye the word which the Lord speaketh unto you, O house of Israel: Thus saith the Lord, Learn not the way of the heathen, and be not dismayed at the signs of heaven; for the heathen are dismayed at them. For the customs of the people are vain: for one cutteth a tree out of the forest, the work of the hands of the workman, with the ax. They deck it with silver and with gold; they fasten it with nails and with hammers that it move not. They are upright as the palm tree, but speak not: they must needs be borne, because they cannot go. Be not afraid of them; for they cannot do evil, neither also is it in them to do good. (Jer. 10:1-5; emphasis added)

Then he brought me to the door of the gate of the LORD's house which was toward the north; and, behold, there sat women weeping for **Tammuz**. *Then said he unto me, Hast thou seen this, O son of man? turn thee yet again, and thou shalt see greater abominations than these. And he brought me into the inner court of the LORD's house, and, behold, at the door of the temple of the LORD, between the porch and the altar, were about five and twenty men, with their backs toward the temple of the LORD, and their faces toward the east; and they* **worshipped the sun** *toward the east. Then he said unto me, Hast thou seen this, O son of man? Is it a light thing to the house of Judah that they commit the abominations which they*

[157]

commit here? for they have filled the land with violence, and have returned to provoke me to anger: and, lo, they put the branch to their nose. Therefore will I also deal in fury: mine eye shall not spare, neither will I have pity: and though they cry in mine ears with a loud voice, yet will I not hear them. (Ezek. 8:14-18; emphasis added)

Upon learning these truths regarding the origin of Christmas and its customs, this year I was led to dispose of every piece of Christmas paraphernalia that I had in my home. Unfortunately, there are many customs and traditions that we tend to accept without question. We never inquire into their origin, view them as harmless, and naturally engage in them. The bottom line however, is not how *we view* a thing but rather what *God* says about it. Thus, it would behoove each of us to seek to understand the origin of many of our *other* commonly held holiday customs and traditions, including Easter. More importantly, we should seek God's guidance on what **He** would have us to do concerning them.

It is interesting to note that many Hebrew Israelites (and others) have categorized Christianity or the Christian faith itself as cultic or a pagan religion. Rightfully, they challenge Christians to research the origin of their faith and particularly the name "Christian," to which they ascribe themselves. However, their foregone conclusion regarding all persons serving God under this title is questionable. No doubt many Hebrew Israelites who cast such a doomsday sentence against Christians, Christianity and/or the Christian faith were in fact themselves

[158]

saved, found Salvation or were "born again" in a "Christian" church (Rom 10:13-15; John 3:3-7; Titus 3:5-7; 1 Pet. 1:22-23). How did that happen, if Christianity or the Christian Faith is totally "of the devil" or paganistic? Similar criticisms have also been waged against the use of the name Jesus versus Yehoshua, (or any other Hebrew variation of the Messiah's name). In answer to this criticism, I ask Hebrew Israelites, before you came into the knowledge of the Messiah's Hebrew name, and you called upon the name of Jesus to save you and you were in fact saved, forgiven of your sins or were *born again*, who heard you? Which saved you? Does it matter? No, because He, the Messiah, knew who you were calling upon. Heard you and saved you—despite using his English name Jesus as opposed to his Hebrew name Yehoshua or any variation thereof.

However, while performing the challenging research regarding the *origin* of the "Christian Faith" I discovered that there are those who actually believe that the "Christian Jesus" is no more than a copycat of the mythological Graeco-Egyptian god Serapis Christus of the 3rd century BC, predating Christ by hundreds of years, or the Indo-Iranian god Mithras, predating Christ by a thousand years or more. Serapis was allegedly called the "Good Shepherd," was considered a healer, was a sacrificial bull as Christ was a sacrificial lamb, and was *annually* sacrificed for the sins of Egypt ("Serapis"). Mithras was *said* to be born of a virgin, was crucified and rose in three days. However, when each of these claims was examined in light of what the myth *actually* says the claims were easily refuted or proven unfounded ("Is Jesus").

What's more, the ultimate source for these claims is said to be a work done by Robert Taylor called *The Diegesis*. Taylor was an early 19th Century Radical and a clergyman turned freethinker. He studied for three years at St John's College, Cambridge to qualify as a clergyman. Five years after his ordination, Taylor gave up on orthodox Christianity and turned from evangelism to eccentric anti-clericalism. He set up a *Christian Evidence Society* and lectured in London pubs, where he attacked the Anglican liturgy and the Establishment for what he called its "Pagan creed." At that time in England, blasphemy was a criminal offence, and he was sentenced to a year in gaol (prison). In his cell he wrote *The Diegesis*, attacking Christianity on the basis of comparative mythology and attempting to explicate it as a scheme of solar myths ("Robert"). However, as stated earlier, alleged similarities of pagan mythology with that of the "Christian" Christ have been refuted or proven unfounded when researched.

Nonetheless, to Hebrew Israelites who are not so ready to discount the "*still*" seeming similarities between the pagan mythological gods and the "Christian Jesus," the author wishes to point out one plausible explanation for the apparent similarities, using the Book of Enoch to do so. This is a book that many Hebrew Israelites are quite familiar with and tend to embrace as sacredly as the canonized scriptures, as others do also.

[160]

In reference to the recorded accounts in Genesis 6:1-4 and the Book of Enoch (6:1-8; 15:1-2), it has been argued that the reason the Watchers or fallen angels *went into* the daughters of men was to corrupt the seed of Woman. It was an attempt on Satan's part to prevent the promised Seed (Jesus/Yehoshua) from coming forth. In the Garden of Eden, God told Satan that He would put enmity between his seed and that of "the woman." Furthermore, her Seed (Jesus/Yehoshua) would cut off his head, and he (Satan) would bruise Christ's heel (Gen. 3:14-15). Thus, Satan used the Watchers or fallen angels to go into the daughters of men to corrupt the seed of Woman in an attempt to prevent God's word from coming to pass. Given this, it might also be argued that Satan used the Watchers or fallen angels to create confusion in the mind of man in an effort to thwart God's redemptive plan for man. The Watchers may have planted fables or pagan myths into men's minds, bearing similarities to the gospel concerning Christ that was yet to be told. Introducing pagan myths thousands or hundreds of years prior to the Gospel that bore similarities to the truth would cause some to doubt the true Gospel when told. Accuse **it** of being a copycat of paganism, judge **it** to be a pagan religion, and wrongly conclude that Christ Himself was a fake or never existed in the first place. The following verses, found in the Book of Enoch seem to give credibility to this argument:

> And I asked the <u>angel</u> who went with me and showed me all <u>the hidden things, concerning that Son of Man</u>, who he was, and whence he

[161]

was, [and] why he went with the Head of
Days? And he answered and said unto me:
This is the son of Man who hath righteousness,
With whom dwelleth righteousness, And who
revealeth all the treasures of that which is
hidden. (Enoch Chapter 46:2; emphasis added)

Thus, according to the book of Enoch, *angels*
had prior and *secret or hidden knowledge* regarding
the Messiah—*who he was,* his origin, *whence he
came*, and why he was with or accompanied the
Head/"Ancient of Days". In addition, note what is
said in Enoch 16:2-3:

And now as to the Watchers who have sent
thee to intercede for them, who had been
[aforetime] in heaven, (say to them): "You
have been in heaven, but [all] the mysteries
had not yet been revealed to you, and you
knew worthless ones, and these in the hardness
of your hearts you have made known to the
women, and through these mysteries women
and men work much evil on earth. (Emphasis
added)

Also, note Enoch 9:6-8:

Thou seest what Azâzêl hath done, who hath
taught all unrighteousness on earth and
revealed the eternal secrets which were
[preserved] in heaven, which men were
striving to learn: And Semjâzâ, to whom Thou
hast given authority to bear rule over his
associates. And they have gone to the
daughters of men upon the earth, and have
slept with the women, and have defiled
themselves, and revealed to them all kinds of
sins. (Emphasis added)

[162]

Again, Satan may have used Watchers or fallen angels to introduce pagan myths into the mind of man that bore similarities to the true gospel concerning Christ thousands or hundreds of years before Jesus/Yehoshua came into the world. This again would create doubt and confusion regarding the gospel when it was heard and cause many to dismiss or relegate it and the Messiah to the status of myth as well.

Besides this, how can any mythological god *predate* Christ who is eternal and was with the Father since the beginning of time (John 1:1-4, 14)? Thus, He existed before any of these mythological gods were even thought of or were possibly planted in the minds of men by Satan and the Watchers or fallen angels. Not only that, Christ was prophetically spoken of throughout the Old Testament, beginning with Genesis and ending with the prophet Malachi, with estimated dates of authorship ranging from 1440 BC to 400 BC. Thus, prophecies were written and recorded about Christ, the coming Messiah, over a thousand years prior to His coming. He was the only one who fulfilled every one of them when He came as flesh more than a thousand years later. So, one has to wonder, who is trying to copy whom?

With respect to the name "Christian," research does find that early believers did not initially call themselves "Christians." A few years following Jesus/Yehoshua's accession, they were first called Christians by non-believing Gentiles in Antioch as a form of mockery (Act 11:26). Early believers called themselves "brethren," "disciples," "saints," "believers," or followers of Christ or the Way (Acts 24:14). The word "Christian" is derived from the Greek word "Chrisitanos" which means "anointed one" or "follower of the anointed one." However, the original Greek word used in the ancient text (Codex Sinaiticus) was "Chrestians" (or "Chrestianos."), which upon research yields various interpretations of its meaning such as "a follower," "a servant of," "a slave of," "a goody-goody," "Christ's crowd," or even perhaps "little Christs." This was the name unbelieving Gentiles in Antioch used in a mocking, contemptible, and derogatory manner to "label" the followers/believers of Christ or the Way" (Luginbill). However, by the 2nd Century AD early believers began calling *themselves* Christians (or Christianos) which they interpreted for themselves to mean "followers of Christ"

Still, many Hebrew Israelites find the name "Christian" objectionable, since it was not a name given to believers by Christ Himself but rather one that believers came to adopt for themselves and one which was derived from a name nonbelievers used in a mocking manner to describe followers of Christ. While it is true that Jesus/Yehoshua never called his disciples or believers "Christians," that "Christian" was a name that Believers later adopted for themselves, which they interpreted to mean "followers of Christ," the aim or objective of early believers was to do and be like Christ. This continues to be the objective of those who hold the title today. Regardless of the title one chooses to ascribe to himself—"Christian," "Believer,"

[164]

"Disciple," or "follower of Christ"—one may argue that the substance is not in the title. The substance is in the heart of the person the title is attempting to describe.[3] However, there may be an exception even to this argument.

If we were to say that words are mere words, therefore the substance is in the heart of a person rather than in a title, we overlook the fact that words (of which titles do consist) have power and substance in and of themselves. Scripture tells us that *"Life and death are in the power of the tongue* (Prov. 18:21). Scripture also tells us that, *"By thy words thou are justified and by thy words thou shalt be condemned"* Matt. 12:37). Therefore, words do have power and substance in themselves. Thus, we may want to take caution the titles we ascribe ourselves, particularly if these titles were not given to us by God but rather the world. As an article I read recently pointed out, by using the world's words rather than God's word to describe ourselves, we may be condemning ourselves unknowingly (Anthony).

This argument would have more validity if the early Believers actually ascribed to themselves the name the unbelieving Gentiles in Antioch gave them in mockery. However, it is understood that this is not the case, as the original name the Gentiles

---

[3] This argument is derived from an article by Richard Anthony, "Should We Call Ourselves a Christian?"—in which he specifically relates that the substance is not in the word "Christian" but rather in the *heart* of the man it [the word "Christian"] is attempting to describe.

gave them was "Chrestians" wherein the name they later ascribed to themselves was "Christians."

One other reason I do not particularly like titles is because titles have certain assumptions affixed to them, often convoluted in nature. For instance, although, in the minds of Christians, *"a Christian"* means "a follower of Christ," in the real and practical sense it means a "follower of the *tenets* of Christianity," which may not necessarily be one and the same—and typically is not. In this sense, one does not have to be a "Christian" to make it into the Kingdom of God. One does, however, have to be a born-again believer in Christ, the Messiah to make it into the Kingdom of God (John 3: 3, 5-7). If being a "Christian" was the required marker to get into the Kingdom, then what of those righteous persons from Adam's generation to Abraham, down to Moses and Malachi's generation, who died in faith or belief before the title "Christian" or the "Christian Faith" ever existed? And what faith and belief did they die in? Simply in faith and belief in a Promised Messiah, that should come into the world to take away the sins of the world (Gen. 3:15, Isa. 7:14; Isa. 9:6-7; Isa. 53: 1-5; Dan. 9:24-26; Heb. 9:13-10:18; Heb.11:13). By the same token, a similar question could be asked of Hebrew Israelites who seek or teach redemption through the Torah in the absence or in the place of Grace or faith. What of those righteous persons from Adam's generation down to Abraham's generation who died in faith or belief *before* the Law or Torah was ever given? According to the scripture, the Law came 430 years *after* the promise (Gal. 3:17).

Additionally, "Christians" have also been criticized by some Hebrew Israelites as being weak or foolish in trying to love and forgive their enemies, particularly their present-day "captors." Some point out that our forefathers knew exactly what to do with our enemies—they destroyed them. Please be reminded that the idea to forgive and to love our enemies did not originate or come from "Christians" or the "Christian Faith." It came directly from Jesus/Yehoshua Himself (Matt. 5:38-48; Matt. 6:14-15; Luke 6:32-36). Furthermore, the Most High told us that vengeance was *His* and that He would repay (Deut. 32:35; Lev. 19:18; Ps. 94:1). As Hebrew Israelites, we should know quite well that vengeance belongs to the Most High God. One need only to look at the biblical accounts of how He served justice against the enemies of Israel throughout bible history to know that He will serve justice against our present enemies as He has promised. However, being no respecter of persons, He will also serve judgment against the unredeemed among Israel as well (Matt. 8:11-12; Luke 13:24-28; Zech. 13:8-9). So in the meantime, let us be reminded that Love never fails (or the law thereof). Now abideth faith, hope, charity, but the greatest of these is charity/love (or the law thereof). And, God is Love (or the giver of the Law thereof).

To the liberty that is afforded me in Christ, knowing that when I walk in love I am fulfilling the Law as the Law instructs me *how* to love the Father and my neighbor or fellowman, I nevertheless have to ask to what degree am I to allow the Father to peel away pagan worldly traditions *and* erroneous

[167]

ideology that I have embraced *as part* of my faith, especially in these last days. This is a question that is not limited just to certain Hebrew Israelites but should be answered by all. As the times of the Gentiles *are* coming to a close, and the Most High begins to re-harness His attention to Israel, the question is no longer "What does He expect of me as an individual?" The question is "What does He expect or require of me as part of a People or a Nation in these last days?" The question is no longer "What does it take for *me* to be blessed?" but rather "What does it take for Us as a *People* to be blessed?" "Being awakened to the truth of my heritage as a Hebrew Israelite, in these last days, what does 'RETURNING' unto Him mean and entail?" We as Hebrew Israelites need to pray and earnestly seek God, the Most High, for the answer to these questions and allow **Him** to lead and direct us. I for one am ready to embrace whatever "Returning unto Him" entails—giving up worldly traditions rooted in paganism, denouncing a false image of Yehoshua, and, yes, even embracing His Seventh-day Sabbath.

As I mentioned from the onset of the book, no one religion or faith has a corner on absolute truth. Every mainstream religion or faith contains a mixture of truth and error, with varying degrees of truth and error within each, but a mixture of truth and error nonetheless. Therefore, it behooves each of us to ask the Most High to reveal *where* those errors are and then cease to embrace them. This critical analysis is not just for those who ascribe to the Christian Faith but to *everyone* of all Faiths. As the times of the Gentiles **are** coming to an end, and God begins to reveal more revelation and more knowledge of TRUTH in these last days, I for one will align myself accordingly, caring not what others have to say about it.

Do not be confused, however; Hebrew Israelite is NOT a faith or a religion. It is a NATIONALITY. It is what a person is by birth, by virtue of being a bloodline descendant of Abraham, Isaac, and Jacob, period. Religion per se is a creation of man and was not the intent or design of God. His design was to prepare a people fitted to live with Him in His Kingdom forever—a Kingdom that is soon to come. However, in order to enter into His Kingdom, scripture tells us that one must be born again (John 3:3, 5). This brings us to our next topic which is the Kingdom of God.

Establishing His Kingdom on the Earth has been God's plan since the beginning of time. As in the parable told by Jesus/Yehoshua, God sent His prophets and servants, then His own Son to invite and prepare people for His coming Kingdom. The prophet Daniel foretold that the saints would eventually possess the Kingdom of God (Dan.7:18, 22, 27). Approximately 600 years after his prophecy, Jesus/Yehoshua came preaching the *gospel of the Kingdom* saying, "*The time is fulfilled, and the kingdom of God is at hand. Repent, and believe in the gospel*'" (Mark 1:14-15). The Kingdom of God was the very heart and core of His message. Thus, the gospel message of Jesus/Yehoshua was not about preparing a people to live in Heaven throughout eternity. His gospel message was about redeeming a people fit to live in the Kingdom of God which would be established forever on the Earth upon His return. It was God's desire and plan all along to establish for Himself a people where He could be their God and they His People. This will be realized when His physical Kingdom—which is soon to come—is established on the Earth, but even more so in the eternal state that is to follow (Rev. 21:1-3).

As an aside, please note that the conception of a "One World" Government and a "New World" Order came from God, not Man or Satan. Having no original thought or idea of his own, Satan takes and perverts God's plan and presents a counterfeit version of his own. Thus, we hear warnings of a "One World Government" and a "New World Order" that is coming upon the peoples of the Earth in the last days. We are told that World leaders are presently engaged in bringing this phenomenon to pass. However, know that the Kingdom of God **IS** the One World Government and the New World Order that WILL MOST ASSUREDLY be established on the Earth, and **It IS** soon to come. Daniel and other Old Testament prophets foretold of God's One World Government and New World Order in scripture.

> *For unto us a child is born, unto us a son is given: and the government SHALL be upon his shoulder: and his name shall be called Wonderful, Counsellor, The mighty God, The everlasting Father, The Prince of Peace. Of the increase of his government and peace there shall be no end, upon the throne of David, and*

upon his kingdom, to order it, and to establish it with judgment and with justice from henceforth even for ever. The zeal of the LORD of hosts will perform this. (Isa. 9:6-7; emphasis added)

And in the days of these kings shall the God of heaven set up a kingdom, which shall never be destroyed: and the kingdom shall not be left to other people, but it shall break in pieces and consume all these kingdoms, and IT shall stand for ever. [The Kingdom of God will thus replace the governments of this world] (Dan. 1:44; emphasis added)

Rejoice greatly, O daughter of Zion; shout, O daughter of Jerusalem: behold, thy King cometh unto thee: he is just, and having salvation; lowly, and riding upon an ass, and upon a colt the foal of an ass. And I will cut off the chariot from Ephraim, and the horse from Jerusalem, and the battle bow shall be cut off: and he shall speak peace unto the heathen: and his dominion shall be from sea even to sea, and from the river even to the ends of the earth. (Zech. 9:9-10; emphasis added)

*And the seventh angel sounded; and there were great voices in heaven, saying, **The kingdoms of this world are become the kingdoms of our Lord, and of his Christ**; and he shall reign for ever and ever.* (Rev. 11:15; emphasis added)

*And he that sat upon the throne said, Behold, **I make ALL things NEW**....* (Rev. 21:5; emphasis added)

Again, the Kingdom of God is the One World Government and the New World order that is to come. Thus, Christ came preaching the gospel message of the Kingdom of God (Matt. 9:35; Matt. 4:17, 23; Mark1:14-15; Luke 9:1-2). It, again, was the very heart and core of His message. He indicated that one of the reasons He was sent was to preach the gospel message of the Kingdom (Luke 4:43). John the Baptist (Matt. 3:1-2), His disciples including Paul (Acts 19:6-8; Acts 20:25; Acts 28:30-31), and Philip the deacon (Acts 8:12) all preached the gospel of the Kingdom of *God.*

The significance of preaching the gospel of the **Kingdom** is reflected in the following scriptures:

> *And this gospel of the kingdom shall be preached in all the world for a witness unto all nations; and then the end shall come.* (Matt. 24:14, emphasis added)

> *But seek ye first the kingdom of God, and his righteousness; and all these things shall be added unto you.* (Matt. 6:33; emphasis added)

Immediately after His resurrection, Jesus taught the disciples for forty days of things *pertaining to the Kingdom of God* (Acts 1:2-3). Finally, the gospel that Jesus commanded *his disciples to preach* during his earthly ministry was the gospel of the *Kingdom of God* (Luke 9:1-2).

So what exactly is the Kingdom of God? Since it was the central focus and core of Jesus/ Yehoshua's gospel message, it seems important that we grasp an understanding of what the Kingdom of God is. One way to clarify what it is is to clarify what it is not. The Kingdom of God is not heaven and it is not the Church. It is not a philosophical or abstract concept that merely resides in the minds of people (Treybig, "Kingdom"). The Kingdom of God is a reality. It is *the rule and reign of God*. It is His sovereignty in action against the *evil in the world*. It is currently not seen but *it is* experienced. It already is, yet is still to come. It is both present and future. It came *as a mystery* in a hidden, *unexpected* form (Naugle). Yet it will be fully manifested in all its glory and physical magnificence when established on the Earth following the second coming. The parables that Jesus/Yehoshua taught His disciples help us understand the mystery of the Kingdom of God and how it has come in this unexpected, but real manner. This is seen through Naugle's synopsis, below, of each parable.

> *The parable of the four soils* (Matt. 13:1-9; 18-23). The Kingdom of God had come but in a hidden and unexpected form. Contrary to standard expectation, it would not be spread by power, but by the **preaching of the Word**. The responses to its message depend upon the conditions of the listeners' hearts. Like seed, it will be received differently by different types of soils or hearts.

> *The parable of the wheat and the tares* (Matt. 13:24-30, 36-43). This parable teaches that the Kingdom is already present in the world. Its coming, however, did not bring about the final separation of the wicked from the righteous. An **intermixture of the good and the evil** will remain in the midst of this present age until Christ returns.

[173]

The parables of the mustard seed and leaven (Matt. 13:31-33). As a mustard seed, the Kingdom of God has entered the world in an imperceptible, humble form and virtually unnoticed. Yet, one day it will be a great tree and encompass the earth. Similarly, the Kingdom of God is hidden as leaven in a lump of dough. It will operate secretly but effectively, and will one day prevail such that no rival kingdom exists.

The parables of the treasure and pearl (Matt. 13:44-46). Because of the Kingdom's inauspicious presence, its importance might be overlooked or despised. However, it is of immeasurable value and ought to be sought above all other possessions. It is humanity's greatest good and is worth selling everything in order to own it.

The parable of the drag-net (Matt. 13:47-50). Virtually identical in meaning to the wheat and the tares, this parable also teaches that the kingdom has come into the world, but without affecting the final judgment. Again, an intermixture of good and evil will remain in the world until Christ returns.

The Kingdom's greatest mystery, however, is connected with the redemptive work of Christ where God in Christ, conquered sin, death, and Satan (Naugle). To become a citizen of the Kingdom of God, Jesus/Yehoshua makes it clear that both Jew and Gentile alike must be born again.

Verily, verily I say unto to thee, Except a man be born again, he cannot see the kingdom of God ... Except a man be born of water and of

[174]

the Spirit, he cannot enter into the kingdom of God... Marvel not that I said unto thee, Ye must be born again. (John 3:3-7)

Thus, entrance into the Kingdom of God is not based on one's natural pedigree. Yet, the Kingdom of God with its physical manifestation on the Earth will be the ultimate fulfillment of the Old Testament promises and blessings of the Covenant that the Most High made to and with (ethnic) Israel.

The Kingdom of God, when literally established on the Earth, will contain the four essential components as are seen in a natural kingdom. It will have a King, Jesus/Yehoshua Himself. It will have a territory, the entire Earth. It will have a people or *citizens*, consisting of both *redeemed* Israelites and Gentiles, where its citizens will reflect the King's nature, values, morals, and culture. The Kingdom of God will also have Laws and a form of government—a theocracy where the absolute Sovereign Will and Law or Word of God will be done and followed. A natural kingdom is *literally* a kingdom (i.e., nation) of people with a distinct culture. This is exactly what the Children or the nation of Israel was **initially** called to be—a Kingdom of priests and a Holy Nation of the Most High God, *distinct* from all the other nations in the Earth.

Now therefore, if ye will obey my voice indeed, and keep my covenant, then ye shall be a peculiar treasure unto me above all people: for all the earth is mine: And ye shall be unto me a kingdom of priests, and an holy nation. These are the words which thou shalt speak unto the

[175]

children of Israel. (Exod. 19:5-6; emphasis added)

Contrary to what is often taught, scripture suggests that, while all citizens of the Kingdom are entitled to, and will enjoy the same benefits of the Kingdom, a *hierarchy* within the Kingdom will nevertheless exist. As has once been noted, the *redeemed* Children or Nation of ethnic Israel will retain their rank and preeminence among the other redeemed nations of the Earth in the Kingdom during the millennium reign. Please note the following scriptures:

> *And the sons of strangers shall build up **thy walls,** and their kings shall minister **unto thee:** for in my wrath I smote thee, but in my favour have I had mercy on thee... For the nation and kingdom **that will not serve thee** shall perish; yea, those nations shall be utterly wasted. . . . and they shall call thee, **The city of the Lord, The Zion of the Holy One of Israel.** Whereas thou has been forsaken and hated, so that no man went through thee, I will make thee **an eternal excellency, a joy of many generations.** (Isa. 60:10, 12, 14-15; emphasis added)*

> *And kings shall be **thy** nursing fathers, and their queens **thy nursing mothers: they shall bow down to thee** with their face toward the earth, and lick up the dust of thy feet, and thou shall know that I am the Lord: for they shall not be ashamed that wait for me. (Isa. 49:23)*

> *And strangers shall stand and feed **your flocks,** and the sons of the alien shall be your plowmen and your vinedressers. **But ye shall be named the Priests of the LORD:** men shall*

[176]

call you the **Ministers of our God:** *ye shall eat the riches of the Gentiles, and in their glory shall ye boast yourselves.* (Isa. 61:5-6; emphasis added)

Israel shall rule the nations.

In that day will I raise up the tabernacle of David that is fallen, and close up the breaches thereof; and I will raise up his ruins, and I will build it as in the days of old: <u>That they may possess the remnant of Edom, and of all the heathen, which are called by my name,</u> *saith the* LORD *that doeth this.* (Amos 9:11-12; emphasis added)

<u>...and the strangers shall be joined with them, and they shall cleave to the house of Jacob. And the people shall take them and bring them, to their place:</u> **and the house of Israel shall possess them** <u>in the land of the</u> LORD <u>for servants and handmaids:...</u> <u>and they shall</u> **rule** <u>over their oppressors.</u> (Isa. 14:1-2; emphasis added)

<u>For the nation and kingdom that will not serve thee shall perish;</u> *yea, those nations shall be utterly wasted.* (Isa. 60:12; emphasis added)

Thus saith the LORD; <u>I am returned unto Zion, and will dwell in the midst of Jerusalem: and Jerusalem shall be called a city of truth; and the mountain of the</u> LORD <u>of hosts the holy mountain...</u> *Thus saith the* LORD *of hosts; It shall yet come to pass, that there shall come people, and the inhabitants of many cities: And the inhabitants of one city shall go to another, saying, Let us go speedily to pray before the* LORD, *and to seek the* LORD *of hosts: I will go also. Yea, many people and strong nations shall come to seek the LORD of hosts in Jerusalem, and to pray before the LORD. Thus saith the LORD of hosts; In those days it shall come to pass, that ten men shall take hold out of all languages of the nations, even shall take hold of the skirt of him that is a Jew, saying, We will go with you: for we have heard that God is with you.* (Zech. 8:3, 20-23; emphasis added)

*And it shall come to pass, that every one that is left of all the nations which came against Jerusalem shall even go up from year to year to worship the King, the LORD of hosts, and to keep the feast of tabernacles. And it shall be, that whoso will not come up of all the families of the earth unto Jerusalem to worship the King, the LORD of hosts, even upon them shall be no rain. And if the family of Egypt go not up, and come not, that have no rain; there shall be the plague, wherewith the LORD will smite **the heathen** that come not up to keep the feast of tabernacles. This shall be the punishment of Egypt, and the punishment of all nations that come not up to keep the feast of tabernacles.* (Zech. 14:16-19; emphasis added)

Disciples will sit on *thrones as Judges*:

... Verily I say unto you, That ye which hath followed me, in the regeneration when the Son of man shall sit in the throne of his glory, ye also shall sit upon twelve thrones, judging the twelve tribes of Israel. (Matt. 19:28; emphasis added)

[178]

*That ye may eat and drink at my table in my
kingdom, <u>and sit on thrones judging the twelve
tribes of Israel.</u>* (Luke 22:30; emphasis added)

Gates of the City are named after the 12 Tribes
of Israel.

*And the gates of the city shall be after the
names of the tribes of Israel: three gates
northward; one gate of Reuben, one gate of
Judah, one gate of Levi. And at the east side
four thousand and five hundred: and three
gates; and one gate of Joseph, one gate of
Benjamin, one gate of Dan And at the south
side four thousand and five hundred measures:
and three gates; one gate of Simeon, one gate
of Issachar, one gate of Zebulun. At the west
side four thousand and five hundred, with their
three gates; one gate of Gad, one gate of
Asher, one gate of Naphtali.* (Ezek. 48:31-34)

Thus, scripture seems to indicate that a
hierarchy will exit within the millennial Kingdom
of God with the redeemed of Israel resuming their
rank or preeminence among the nations, including
being caretakers and carriers of God's Word to the
nations, once again (Zech. 8:20-23). For now,
however, the plan has been reversed.

*Even us, whom he hath called, not of the Jews
only, but also of the Gentiles? As he saith also
in Osee, <u>I will call them my people, which were
not my people; and her beloved, which was not
beloved.</u> And it shall come to pass, that in the
place where it was said unto them, Ye are not
my people; there shall they be called the
children of the living God. Esaias also crieth
concerning Israel, Though the number of the*

[179]

children of Israel be as the sand of the sea, a
remnant shall be saved: For he will finish the
work, and cut it short in righteousness:
because a short work will the Lord make upon
the earth. (Rom 9:24-28; emphasis added)

Thus, instead of the nation of Israel converting Gentiles, the Gentiles accepted Israel's rejected Redeemer and, for the most part, now lead Israel or Jacob's seed to their Messiah. In so doing "all believing" Israelites will be saved (Rom 11:23, 25-27). In the last days, however, the plan will revert back to Israel to teach the nations *for the gifts and calling of God are without repentance* (Kelly; Rom. 11:29)

In those days it shall come to pass, that ten
men shall take hold out of all languages of the
nations, even shall take hold of the skirt of him
that is a Jew, saying, "We will go with you: for
we have heard that God is with you. (Zech.
8:23; emphasis added)

And many people shall go and say, Come ye,
and let us go up to the mountain of the LORD,
to the house of the God of Jacob; and he will
teach us of his ways, and we will walk in his
paths: for out of Zion shall go forth the law,
and the word of the LORD *from Jerusalem.*
(Isa. 2:3; emphasis added)

Habakkuk himself knew that God had chosen his nation centuries earlier to accomplish a special mission. In light of this, he did not understand why God would allow catastrophe to occur to Judah, especially at the hands of a nation *"more wicked"* than they. God assured Habakkuk, however, that He would accomplish His purpose with Judah but that it would be ***at a later time.*** God also told the prophet that he must *wait for the time of HIS choosing* to bring it to pass. In the meantime, God reminded Habakkuk that "the just shall live by his faith" ("Why Don't"; emphasis added).

Chapter Three:
In Defense of God

In the final analysis, when all is said and done, it has been God, the Most High, who has gotten the short end of the stick throughout all of humanity. In the Supreme Courtroom of Justice, we all stand guilty before Him—all nations, all races, and all kindred of people. Each one of us is guilty of falling short of His Glory and the honor that is due Him. And what did He desire of His Creation and of Man whom He created in His Own Image and for His Glory? Nothing, except for man to walk circumspectly before Him and to freely give to Him the Glory, Praise, and Honor that is due Him as Father, God, and Creator of the Universe. When the first Man (or couple) *essentially* failed in doing this, He promised to send the seed of the Woman—the promised Messiah, to redeem man and His creation from the curse of the fall and back to Himself (Gen. 3:15). When the wickedness of man later rose to such heights that He even repented of having made man, God destroyed all of mankind with a flood save *one righteous family*—Noah, his wife, his three sons and their wives (Gen. 6:6-8; 7:7). The Almighty later chose a nation out of all the nations in the Earth through which to send the Messiah so that all the families of the Earth might be blessed through a covenant He made with Abraham (Gen. 12:1-3).

[182]

The Most High chose the Nation of Israel as that nation and as His special people unto Himself through which to send the Messiah. In order to save or purchase Man's redemption or redeem Man back to God, according to the Law (i.e. the Law of Redemption), Messiah had to be related to or kin to Man to become his Kinsmen Redeemer (Lev. 25: 23-28). So, He had to be born after the flesh and thus related to Man to purchase his redemption   He also *had* to come in the flesh and in the likeness of sinful flesh to condemn sin in the flesh (Rom. 8:3-4). Consequently, *a people* had to be chosen through which the Messiah, the savior and redeemer of the World, would come. *God chose* the nation of Israel through which the Messiah would and did come. One might ask why God chose Israel as opposed to any other nation. Besides the fact that God is God and Sovereign and can do or choose whomsoever He desires for whatever purpose He has, another explanation is offered in the following scripture of Deuteronomy 7:6-9.

> *For thou art an holy people unto the LORD thy God: the LORD thy God hath* chosen thee to be a special people unto himself, *above all people that are upon the face of the earth.* The LORD did not set his love upon you, nor choose you, because ye were more in number than any people; for ye were the fewest of all people: But because the LORD loved you, and because he would keep the oath *which he had sworn unto your fathers,* hath the LORD *brought you out with a mighty hand, and redeemed you out of the house of bondmen, from the hand of Pharaoh king of Egypt. Know therefore that*

[183]

the LORD thy God, he is God, the faithful God,
which keepeth covenant and mercy with them
that love him and keep his commandments to a
thousand generation;

Thus, God chose Israel because He promised *Abraham* that he and his descendants would become a great nation (Gen. 12:1-3, 5-7). God later repeated the promise to Abraham (Gen. 13:14-18; 17:1-9, 19-21; Gen. 22:15-18) and then to Abraham's descendants (26:1-5, 17, 24; 28:10-16). Abraham and his descendants were blessed accordingly because of Abraham's *faith and his obedience to God.*

And I will make thy seed to multiply as the
stars of heaven, and will give unto thy seed all
these countries; <u>and in thy seed shall all the</u>
<u>nations of the earth be blessed;</u> **Because** *<u>that</u>*
<u>Abraham obeyed</u> my voice, <u>and kept my</u>
<u>charge, my commandments, my statutes, and</u>
<u>my laws.</u> (Gen. 26:4-5; emphasis added)

As an aside, another interesting question one might ask is, why did God chose *Abraham* from among all the peoples of the Earth in which to enter into an everlasting covenant? The book of Jubilees provides us with the insight that God chose Abraham because Abraham chose Him.

And it came to pass in the sixth week, in the seventh year thereof [1904 A.M.], that Abram said to Terah his father, saying, "Father!" And he said, "Behold, here am I, my son." And he said "What help and profit have we from those idols which thou dost worship, And before which thou dost bow thyself? For there is no spirit in them, For they are dumb forms, and a misleading of the heart. Worship them not: Worship the God of heaven, Who causes the rain and the dew to descend on the earth And does everything upon the earth, And has created everything by His word, And all life is from before His face. Why do ye worship things that have no spirit in them? For they are the work of [men's] hands, And on your shoulders do ye bear them, And ye have no help from them, But they are a great cause of shame to those who make them, And a misleading of the heart to those who worship them: Worship them not." And his father said unto him, "I also know it, my son, but what shall I do with a people who have made me to serve before them? And, if I tell them the truth, they will slay me; for their soul cleaves to them to worship them and honour them. Keep silent, my son, lest they slay thee." And these words he spake to his two brothers, and they were angry with him and he kept silent. (Jubilees 12:1-8)

And in the sixth week, in the fifth year thereof, [1951 A.M.] Abram sat up throughout the night on the new moon of the seventh month to observe the stars from the evening to the morning, in order to see what would be the character of the year with regard to the rains, and he was alone as he sat and observed. And a word came into his heart and he said: "All the signs of the stars, and the signs of the moon and of the sun are all in the hand of the Lord. Why do I search (them) out? If He desires, He causes it to rain, morning and evening; And if He desires, He withholds it, And all things are

[185]

in his hand." And he prayed that night and said, "My God, God Most High, Thou alone art my God, And Thee and Thy dominion have I chosen. And Thou hast created all things, And all things that are the work of thy hands. Deliver me from the hands of evil spirits who have dominion over the thoughts of men's hearts, And let them not lead me astray from Thee, my God. And stablish Thou me and my seed for ever. That we go not astray from henceforth and for evermore." And he said, "Shall I return unto Ur of the Chaldees who seek my face that I may return to them, am I to remain here in this place? The right path before Thee prosper it in the hands of Thy servant that he may fulfil [it] and that I may not walk in the deceitfulness of my heart, O my God."

And he made an end of speaking and praying, and behold the word of the Lord was sent to him through me, saying: "Get thee up from thy country, and from thy kindred and from the house of thy father unto a land which I will show thee, and I shall make thee a great and numerous nation. And I will bless thee And I will make thy name great, And thou shalt be blessed in the earth, And in Thee shall all families of the earth be blessed, And I will bless them that bless thee, And curse them that curse thee. And I will be a God to thee and thy son, and to thy son's son, and to all thy seed: fear not, from henceforth and unto all generations of the earth I am thy God. (Jubilee 12:16-24)

Thus, God's primary reason for choosing the Nation of Israel as his special people was to bring the Messiah, Jesus/Yehoshua into the world. While this was his ultimate purpose, it was not his sole purpose. Israel was also chosen to be "a kingdom of priests and a holy nation", distinct from the other nations in the Earth, to reflect the nature, values, and morals of the Most High God (Exod. 19:6; Isa. 51:4). They were to teach other nations about Him and point them towards His promised provision of the Redeemer, Messiah, and Savior ("Why Did"). He wanted Israel to be an example to other nations, to show that, when a nation obeyed Him, that nation would be blessed (Treybig, "Why"). However, for the most part, Israel failed miserably at their task and thus reaped a history of judgments against them rather than God's blessings.

The things we as Blacks have suffered during slavery and in our present-day captivity have been atrocious. There is no doubt about it. From rapes, castrations, mutilations, brutal beatings, and lynchings to oppression, discrimination, Jim Crow laws, and government-supported inhumane experimentations; the list continues from bombings, church burnings, police brutality, and killings, and an unjust criminal-justice system to physical and psychological genocide. It may do us well to some degree however, to review some of the things our forefathers did that resulted in God's judgment against them. We may find that some of the atrocities our forefathers committed are not too unlike those that are being done against us today. *Every* nation over the course of history has committed grave atrocities against other nations, against themselves, and against God, including Israel and Judah. No nation (or person, for that matter) stands guilt free before the Most High and Almighty God in its or their own right.

God, through Amos, pronounced judgments against eight nations of his day. Judah and Israel were among those nations. Each nation—Damascus, Gaza, Tyrus, Edom, Moab, Ammon, Judah, and Israel—stood guilty of grievous sins before God. *Damascus* for the cruel punishment they used against the people of Gilead. They tore their bodies with threshing instruments. Gaza stood guilty and was judged for selling Israelites into slavery to Edom. God judged *Tyrus* for breaking their *brotherly covenant* with Israel and for selling them as slaves to the Edomites. *Edom* was judged for his on-going hatred and revengeful spirit against his brother Jacob/Israel. He perpetually pursued Jacob with anger and wrath, even to this day. *Moab* was judged for carrying their revenge against Edom too far. They burned the King of Edom's bones to lime. *Ammon* was judged because they ripped open the women with child at Gilead to enlarge their borders (Gill; Amos 1:1-15).

Many injustices were also committed by **our** forefathers in the Southern Kingdom of Judah. The wealthy oppressed the poor and took away their houses and land. They pillaged and plundered the poor of all they had and left them as bare as bones stripped of their flesh by placing heavy taxes, levies, exorbitant penalties, and fines upon them (Gill; Mic. 3:2-3). They perverted the rules and laws

[188]

of justice and equity, clearing the guilty and condemning the innocent for the right price. *They build up Zion with blood, and Jerusalem with iniquity.* Thus, they built themselves stately houses or large streets with monies they took of murderers they had saved or by oppression and spoiling the poor of their goods and livelihood and by shedding innocent blood (Gill; Mic. 3:9-10).

Similarly in the Northern Kingdom of Israel, the rich oppressed the poor and became richer. They were lovers of money and full of greed. They were heartless in their treatment of the poor, making them pay dearly for their provisions by which they were not able to support themselves and their families. The Northern Kingdom also failed to administer justice fairly. Instead, justice was perverted and corrupted. Judges or law official fined men unjustly. The innocent were judged guilty for a bribe. Business practices were also corrupt. Scales and balances were falsified by deceit contrary to God's Law (Deut. 25:13-15). They sold refuse (i.e., chaff of the wheat that was swept off the floor) or inferior grain to the poor at a very high price—grain that was not fit to make bread but was only fit for cattle. Murder, theft and perjury were common occurrences (Gill; Amos 2:6-8; 8:4-6).

Sexual immorality was to such degree that a man and his father went *in to the same maiden.* Though they attended the holy feast days, they had no real thought of God. They could not wait for the feast days to end so they could return to the business of making more money. As sated before, they despised God's Law (Gill; Amos 2:7; 8:5).

[189]

Not excluded from deeds of wickedness were the Kings of both Judah and Israel. Throughout their history, all were primarily evil. During its history, the Northern Kingdom had nineteen Kings. ALL were evil except one. Jehu was characterized as "mixed," being both good and evil. The Southern Kingdom of Judah had twenty Kings, of which twelve of them were evil. Two began their reign as good Kings but were characterized as evil in their old age. Thus, only six of Judah's twenty Kings were considered good kings before God. The sins of these various kings included, murder to secure another man's property or the throne itself, sacrificing via fire their own children to idol gods, idolatry and sexual immorality including adultery. Such evil and sinful leadership came from a people whom God had delivered with a mighty hand from Egyptian bondage and had set aside as a Chosen People unto himself, provided for and protected (destroying their enemies), and brought safely to their promised land. What an affront to a merciful God!

However, perhaps the most despicable time period in Israel's history was the time of Judges—when Israel had no king, and *every man did that which was right in his own eyes*" (Judg. 17:6; 21:25). During this time, Israelites committed such acts as murder, including brothers killing brothers and gang rape resulting in death. Homosexuality was also named among the Israelites (Judg. 19:1-21, 25). Israel had completely ignored God's way and instead chose to go their own way, not unlike many Hebrew Israelites today. In our Hebrew Israelite

[190]

communities, what do we find? A high rate of Hebrew Israelites killing other Hebrew Israelites, a high rate of spousal abuse, a high rate of drug abuse, a high rate of absentee fathers, a high rate of divorce and homosexuality, a high rate of teenage pregnancy, a high rate of abortions and the list goes on. However, in the following scriptures we see how the Most High God desired His people Israel to treat and honor one another. They were to serve as an example to the other nations who knew not the God of Israel. Compare the beauty of the relationship that God desired that we have with how we are actually living and treating one another as a people today.

And when ye reap the harvest of your land, thou shalt not wholly reap the corners of thy field, neither shalt thou gather the gleanings of thy harvest. And thou shalt not glean thy vineyard, neither shalt thou gather every grape of thy vineyard; thou shalt leave them for the poor and stranger: I am the LORD your God. Ye shall not steal, neither deal falsely, neither lie one to another. And ye shall not swear by my name falsely, neither shalt thou profane the name of thy God: I am the LORD. Thou shalt not defraud thy neighbour, neither rob him: the wages of him that is hired shall not abide with thee all night until the morning. Thou shalt not curse the deaf, nor put a stumblingblock before the blind, but shalt fear thy God: I am the LORD. Ye shall do no unrighteousness in judgment: thou shalt not respect the person of the poor, nor honor the person of the mighty: but in righteousness shalt thou judge thy neighbour. Thou shalt not

[191]

go up and down as a talebearer among thy *people:* neither shalt thou stand against the blood of thy neighbour; I am the LORD. *Thou* *shalt not hate thy brother in thine heart: thou* *shalt in any wise rebuke thy neighbour, and* *not suffer sin upon him. Thou shalt not avenge,* *nor bear any grudge against the children of* *thy people, but thou shalt love thy neighbour* *as thyself: I am the LORD.* (Lev. 19 9-18; emphasis added)

If there be among you a poor man of one of thy *brethren within any of thy gates in thy land* *which the LORD thy God giveth thee, thou shalt* *not harden thine heart, nor shut thine hand* *from thy poor brother: But thou shalt open* *thine hand wide unto him, and shalt surely* *lend him sufficient for his need, in that which* *he wanteth. Beware that there be not a thought* *in thy wicked heart, saying, The seventh year,* *the year of release, is at hand; and thine eye be* *evil against thy poor brother, and thou givest* *him nought; and he cry unto the LORD against* *thee, and it be sin unto thee. Thou shalt surely* *give him, and thine heart shall not be grieved* *when thou givest unto him:* because that for *this thing the LORD thy God shall bless thee in* *all thy works, and in all that thou puttest thine* *hand unto. For the poor shall never cease out* *of the land: therefore I command thee, saying,* *Thou shalt open thine hand wide unto thy* *brother, to thy poor, and to thy needy, in thy* *land.* (Deut. 15:7-11; emphasis added)

And if thy brother be waxen poor, and fallen in *decay with thee; then thou shalt relieve him:* *yea, though he be a stranger, or a sojourner;* *that he may live with thee. Take thou no usury of him, or increase: but fear thy God; that thy brother may live with thee. Thou shalt not give him thy money upon usury, nor lend him thy victuals for increases. I am the* LORD *your God, which brought you forth out of the land of Egypt, to give you the land of Canaan, and to be your God.*

And if thy brother that dwelleth by thee be waxen poor, and be sold unto thee; <u>*thou shalt not compel him to serve as a bondservant: But as an hired servant,*</u> *and as a sojourner, he shall be with thee, and shall serve thee unto the year of jubile. And then shall he depart from thee, both he and his children with him, and shall return unto his own family, and unto the possession of his fathers shall he return.* <u>*For they are my servants, which I brought forth out of the land of Egypt: they shall not be sold as bondmen. Thou shalt not rule over him with rigour; but shalt fear thy God.*</u>

<u>*Both thy bondmen, and thy bondmaids, which thou shalt have, shall be of the heathen that are round about you; of them shall ye buy bondmen and bondmaids. Moreover of the children of the strangers that do sojourn among you,*</u> **<u>*of them*</u>** <u>*shall ye buy, and of their families that are with you, which they begat in your land: and they shall be your possession. And ye shall take*</u> **<u>*them*</u>** <u>*as an inheritance for your children after you, to inherit them for a possession;*</u> **<u>*they shall be your bondmen for ever:*</u>** <u>*but*</u> **<u>*over your brethren the children of Israel,*</u>** <u>*ye shall*</u> **<u>*not*</u>** <u>*rule one over another with rigour.*</u> (Lev. 25:35-46; emphasis added)

[193]

Thou shalt not lend upon usury [i.e., interest] *to thy brother; usury of money, usury of victuals, usury of any thing that is lent upon usury: Unto a stranger thou mayest lend upon usury; but unto thy brother thou shalt not lend upon usury: that the LORD thy God may bless thee in all that thou settest thine hand to in the land whither thou goest to possess it. When thou comest into thy neighbour's vineyard, then thou mayest eat grapes thy fill at thine own pleasure; but thou shalt not put any in thy vessel. When thou comest into the standing corn of thy neighbour, then **thou mayest pluck the ears with thine hand**; but thou shalt not move a sickle unto thy neighbour's standing corn.* (Deut. 23:19-25; emphasis added)

When the LORD thy God shall bring thee into the land whither thou goest to possess it, and hath cast out many nations before thee, the Hittites, and the Girgashites, and the Amorites, and the Canaanites, and the Perizzites, and the Hivites, and the Jebusites, seven nations greater and mightier than thou; And when the LORD thy God shall deliver them before thee; thou shalt smite them, and utterly destroy them; thou shalt make no covenant with them, nor shew mercy unto them: Neither shalt thou make marriages with them; thy daughter thou shalt not give unto his son, nor his daughter shalt thou take unto thy son. For they will turn away thy son from following me, that they may serve other gods: so will the anger of the LORD be kindled against you, and destroy thee suddenly. (Deut. 7:1-4; emphasis added)

After reading these scriptures, it should become readily and painfully apparent just how far we as Hebrew Israelites are from the culture, the values, the morals and the way of life the Most High, God intended for His people and just how far we are from the amicable and honorable relationship He intended the Israelites to have with one another.

It should also be apparent how all nations of the Earth have sinned and come short of the glory of God. However, God offers each person and nation, grace through redemption in Yehoshua/Christ Jesus, if such grace is accepted, proving that He is not only God of the Jews but God of the Gentiles as well. In the end, every nation (Jew and Gentile nations alike) will have to answer to Him and Him alone (Rom. 3:23-30; 2 Cor. 5:10).

However, make no mistake about it. God did choose Israel as His own special people. He established Himself as their God and delivered them with a Mighty Hand from their (first) Egyptian bondage. He protected them, loved them, and cared for them as a hen careth for her young. He forgave them of their spiritual adultery and idolatry as they hungered and desired to be like "the other nations" around them. However, being a *stiffnecked, backsliding* people, who repeatedly disobeyed God, they, rather than reaping the promised blessings of the Covenant, reaped the curses instead—and thus a history of judgment and enslavements. God used select nations as instruments of judgment and punishment against the Children of Israel for their repeated disobedience to Him (Deut. 28:15, 47-50; Isa. 42:24-25). First there were the Babylonian and

[195]

Assyrian captivities, followed by the Persian, Greek, and Roman dominations and/or persecutions. Having been scattered throughout various lands, the bloodline descendants of Jacob are currently experiencing the covenant curses in their present-day captivity *in the lands of their enemies*. Our present-day captivity or exile is no different from that of our forefathers' who brought God's judgment and covenant curses upon us due to repeated disobedience to Him. Of a surety, however, those nations that God used to bring judgment against us will also be judged and judged in the manner He deemed they would be judged (Isa. 60:10, 12, 14; Isa.14:1-2; Jer. 30:16; Zech. 12:9; Joel 3:2, 7; Rev. 13:10).

Albeit, we cannot blame God or any of the nations HE used to punish us for our and our forefathers' repeated disobedience to Him. As a people, we in part are responsible for our ongoing cursed condition, and ONLY WE can do something about it—not by gaining more worldly education, not by gaining worldly economic independence, nor by gaining an increase in worldly wealth. Though these things have a rightful place in our lives, they are NOT the means to our deliverance as a people. The Most High God would not have it so. We as His ethnic chosen People must RETURN unto Him and look to Him and HIM ALONE for our total deliverance. Please do not view and discredit this remedy to our situation as being weak and conciliatory. It is NOT. It is more powerful than the natural mind can comprehend. As a Nation of People, we cannot be redeemed from the covenant curses by any *man or by human effort*. The Most High has deemed it so; "...and *No man shall buy or save"* us. Our redemption (as a Nation of People) will only come by the hand of the Most High Himself and only when we, as a People, His Chosen Ones, meet the necessary conditions God requires for such redemption and restoration to take place, HENCE Deuteronomy 30:1-3:

> *And it shall come to pass, when ALL these things are come upon thee, the blessing and the CURSE, which I have set before thee, and thou shalt CALL them to mind among all the nations, whither the LORD thy God hath driven thee, And shalt* **RETURN** *unto the LORD thy God, and shalt OBEY his voice according to all that I command thee this day, **thou and thy children,** with all thine heart, and with all thy soul; That **then** the LORD THY GOD will turn thy captivity, and have compassion upon thee, and WILL RETURN and gather thee from all the nations, whither the LORD thy God hath scattered thee.* (Emphasis added)

Howbeit, in the final analysis, when ALL is said and done, remember: in God's eyes, no nation— absolutely *No nation*— can glory *in itself* or point an accusing finger at the other. No nation— absolutely *no nation*— will escape the punishment it deserves and SHALL receive in the end. No nation—absolutely NO NATION—shall have earned the Mercy that God may show it in the end. For in the end... It is **He** who will have mercy on whom He **will** have mercy.

[197]

Chapter Four:
The Conclusion of the Matter

God is Creator and Master of the Universe. He is the maker of all mankind and is the One and Only One True God that is sovereign over all the Earth and the Universe. He hath made of *one* blood *all* nations of men to dwell on all the face of the Earth and hath determined the times before appointed and the bounds of their habitation. He determined, before the foundations of the world, which nations would exist, for what periods of time they should exist, and also their rise and their fall (Acts 17:26-27; Psalm 75:7). He even determined beforehand the years, months, and days of every man's life (Job 7:1). He *is* God, and World History is HIS STORY unfolding before man. Redeeming Man and preparing a people fitted to live with Him forever in His Kingdom is focal to that history. Throughout the ages, He has always reserved a "righteous" remnant in order to carry out His plan of redemption for Man and through which the seed of the Woman, the Savior of the World, would be born. When Adam fell, He reserved Noah and his family ultimately for this reason. He later chose the Children or the Nation of Israel to be a nation and a people unto Himself—through whom the Promised Savior of the world did come. These people were Hebrew Israelites, bloodline descendants of Abraham, Isaac, and Jacob with whom He entered into an everlasting covenant. Hebrew Israelites, which archeological, historical, genetic, and, more importantly, biblical evidence show were people of color whose skin coloring was the same as the Ancient Egyptians—black.

Now, for those who argue that color or race does not or should not matter, you are absolutely right. Color should NOT matter but, evidently, at one point it DID and still does. It mattered to those who went through such great pains to whitewash Black biblical icons and repaint them and the image of Christ into *their own likeness* rather than present Him and the ancient Hebrew Israelites to the world as He and they were presented in the earliest ancient depictions of them found in the Catacombs of Rome—as a man and a people of color. You are right. To *God,* color *Did Not Matter* when choosing a nation through whom He would bring the Savior of the World. Color was *not* an issue for HIM. However, for those who had the power to write and rewrite history, color *did* matter. For those who benefitted from such actions and continue to benefit, color did and still does matter. Absolutely, color was *not* an issue or a matter with GOD. However, MAN with his OWN agenda **made** it a MATTER to the degree of trying to re-write history and falsify Truth. How egregious was and is man to take the plan of God, usurp and distort it just to promote or aggrandize himself, his race, and own agenda, be he Jew or Gentile.

To be clear, Gentiles throughout history are guilty of this very thing. However, the flipside of this is also occurring among Hebrew Israelites. As many come into the knowledge of their true identity, we witness the aggrandizing of Hebrew Israelites to the debasement of all others. However, hear ye, O Israel, adopt not the ways of *"the heathen"* nor fall into the same trap as *"our enemies"* but know this: With God, it was never about Power and Race but about Principle and Grace. Color did (and does not) matter to God, but character does; which is probably why in His omniscience He chose Jacob through which to establish His Godly legacy rather than Esau.

Today, race matters to the degree that TRUTH matters. And the truth of the matter is that the ancient Hebrew Israelites were people of color and still are today. They are the bloodline descendants of Abraham, Isaac, and Jacob, to whom God entered into an everlasting covenant. They are the ones who, because of their repeated disobedience and failure to keep God's laws and statutes, reaped (and continue to reap) the curses of the Covenant as God forewarned. They were the ones who fell victim to the transatlantic (and Indian Ocean) slave trade and were scattered *via ships* throughout the four corners of the Earth and sold as *bondmen and bondwomen* as God forewarned. Their descendants are now known as African Americans, Hattians, Jamaicans, and Dominicans, to name a few.

In the infamous Willie Lynch letter (whether one believes it to be authentic or fabricated) the following *is* written:

> ....more recently we stated that, by reversing
> the positions of the male and female savages,

[200]

we created an orbiting cycle that turns on its own axis forever *unless a phenomenon occurred* and resift [the] positions of the male and female savages. *Our experts warned us about the possibility of this phenomenon occurring,* for they say that the *mind has a strong drive to correct and re-correct itself over a period of time if* [it] *can touch some substantial original historical base,* and they advised us that the best way to deal with the phenomenon is to *shave off the brute's mental history and create a multiplicity of phenomena of illusions,* so that each illusion will twirl in its own obit something similar to floating balls in a vacuum (Lynch; emphasis added).

Denying truth and re-writing World *and* American History was a strategy used to shave off the enslaved Hebrew Israelite's mental history of his or her true heritage and identity. Their history became in their minds whatever the slave master or the "history" books told them their history was. The multiplicity of illusions controlled through media outlets and social oppression, reinforced the false mental history of the Hebrew Israelites. But, alas, over a period of time the forewarned *phenomenon* has occurred, as the Hebrew Israelites, by the will, hand, and timing of God have touched on some *substantial original historical base* of who they are from the very Word of God. Through scripture, we know that the Hebrew Israelites were God's chosen people (Deut. 7:6; Deut. 14:2; Deut. 32:8-9; 2 Sam. 7:23-24; 1 Kings 8:53; 1 Chron. 17:20-21; Ps. 105:6 Ps. 135:4; Isa. 41:8-9; Isa. 44:21; Isa. 48:12). Through Scripture, we know that God entered into an everlasting covenant with them including their future descendants (Gen. 17:7-8; Gen. 28:13-14; Gen. 35:11-12; Gen. 48:3-4). Through scripture, we know that they stood at the foot of Mount Sinai and received the Commandments of God written by the hand of God (Exod. 19:10-13, 17; Exod. 20:1-18; Lev. 27:34). Through scripture, we know that God set before them both blessings and curses based on their obedience or disobedience to the Covenant agreement (Deut.11:26-28; Deut. 28: 1-3, 15; Deut. 30:15-19). Through scripture, we know that they vowed to keep all the statutes, laws and commandments of the Covenant God gave them (Exod. 19:7-8; Exod. 24:7-8). Throughout scripture we know they failed miserably time and time again in keeping this Covenant. Through scripture we know that one of the curses in failing to keep all the statutes, laws, and commandments of the Covenant would be the scattering of them to the four corners of the Earth *via ships* to be sold as bondmen and bondwomen (Deut.28:64, 68). Through scripture, we know that, because of their disobedience and repeated failure to keep God's covenant, they were in fact scattered to the four corners of the Earth (Deut. 28:49, 64; Isa. 42:24-25; Ezek. 39:23-24. 27-28) via a confederacy (Psalm 83:1-8; Joel 3:3-7) and via ships (Deut. 28:68) and sold as bondmen and bondwomen (Deut. 28:68; Joel 3:3, 5-6).

Through scripture, as well as through archeological, historical, and genetic evidence, we know that the descendants of the ancient Hebrew Israelites who fell victim to the slave trade and were scattered throughout the four corners of the Earth

[202]

are now known as African Americans, Hattians, Jamaicans, and Dominicans, to name a few. ("A Western Misrepresentation of the Jews" by Abolitionist; *From Babylon to Timbuktu* by Rudolph Windsor; map of the Kingdom of Juda (Judah) in West Africa in Guinea Slave Coast; I Maccabee 3:48; Wisdom of Solomon 4:15-21; Foreign Relations Document, volume E-5, documents on Africa 1969-1972;. "Igbo People in the Atlantic Slave Trade"; *Murder at Montpelier: Igbo Africans in Virginia.* p 23; "A Brief History of the Terms for Jew," *Jewish Almanac* 1980, p 3; Deut. 28:49, 64, 68; Lev. 26; "Nigeria," *Jewish Virtual Library*; Trans-Atlantic Slave Trade Data Base; Gen. 10:1-5; Gen.10:6-20; Gen. 9:18-19; Ps. 83:1-8; Joel 3:1-7; Isa. 42: 22, 24-25; *Zondervan Compact Bible Dictionary* p. 213; *Young's Bible Dictionary*, p 255-256; "The Bantu Branch of 'Africans' are Hebrew Israelites PART II" by Aria Nasi; *Facts are Facts* by Benjamin Freeman; *The Zionist Connection II,* by Alfred M. Lilienthal).

The covenant curses and the nations that enslaved and oppressed the Hebrew Israelites were but instruments God used to judge and punish His chosen but disobedient people. However, as the *times of the Gentiles* are coming to an end, it is time for Hebrew Israelites to awaken to who they are. You are "Yisrael," God's Chosen People with whom He made an everlasting covenant and promise. This is your roots and this is your heritage. This Truth must be taught to the next generation. Our children must know who they are and know their rich heritage.

[203]

Just because Hebrew Israelites, for the most part, do not know who they are or know their biblical heritage does not mean others do not know. In fact, other nations are more aware of who true Israel is than Hebrew Israelites themselves. Remember, our history and heritage was hidden from **us** by the providence of God. It was not necessarily hidden from other nations. God said *we* would be *cut off* from and be *partially blinded* to our heritage due to our ancestors' repeated disobedience to him. Therefore, other nations had and still have knowledge of who we are and know who we are.

Additionally, many, if not all, benefit from *our* lack of knowledge of who we are, lest we rise and unite in return and repentance to our God to our deliverance and their demise according to scripture (Deut. 30:1-3, 5-7; 1 Kings 8:46-51; Rom. 11:26–27; Jer. 30:11, 20-21; Isa. 49:23, 25-26). Thus, they (i.e. the powers that be) are hard pressed to KEEP us in the dark concerning our true identity and do so in any way or by whatever means necessary. Therein do they promote a particular image and present lies about who we are. Therein do they present a false re-written history of who we are and take every opportunity to denigrate and distort who we are. You are not gang bangers; you are not thugs; you are not drug dealers or users; you are not criminals or abusers of one another; and you are not homosexuals or adulterers. You are Israel—God's Chosen People—the bloodline descendants of Abraham, Isaac, and Jacob. You do not need permission from ANYONE to accept this truth. You

[204]

need only to accept it for YOURSELF. Seek GOD for this Truth. Take no man's word for this. Not even mine. Pray, Research, and Seek the MOST HIGH for Yourselves. He will reveal it to *YOU*!

We have received from God, His mighty hand of judgment as we have endured the covenant curses for nearly 400 years as a people. Remember, not knowing who we are, was part of the curse *until* the times of the Gentiles be fulfilled (Rom. 11:25). It is now time to awaken. The time of Our Great Awakening prophesied in Duet 30:1-3 has come. It is taking place even at this very moment in time. It is imperative that we awaken, as we are quickly approaching the end times. However, to awaken to whom we are as Hebrew Israelites *is not* to awaken to worldly racial pride, haughtiness, or hatred. It is to awaken to TRUTH and the rich heritage that is ours as a People. It is to awaken to humility and yet to a strong resolve to seek the God of our forefathers in repentance and RETURN unto HIM. It is to awaken to the truth that we are a destined people through the Covenant Promises of God *and* through the redemptive work of Jesus/Yehoshua by faith. It is to awaken to the need for *collective* repentance and to allow God to thoroughly purge **us** from every form of idolatry and worldly tradition not pleasing unto Him so as to fulfill the mandate given us (Exod. 19:6; Lev. 20:26). It is to awaken to an assurance that the Promises made to us will be fulfilled according to His Will and according to the Everlasting Covenant He made with our forefathers, Abraham, Isaac, and Jacob.

*And I will set my glory among the heathen, and all the heathen shall see my judgment that I have executed, and my hand that I have laid upon them. So the house of Israel shall know that I am the LORD their God from that day and forward. And the heathen shall know that the <u>house of Israel went into captivity for their iniquity: because they trespassed against me, therefore hid I my face from them, and gave them into the hand of their enemies: so fell they all by the sword. According to their uncleanness and according to their transgressions have I done unto them</u>, and hid my face from them. <u>Therefore thus saith the Lord GOD; Now will I bring again the captivity of Jacob, and have mercy upon the whole house of Israel,</u> and will be jealous for my holy name; **After** <u>that they have borne their shame, and all their trespasses whereby they have trespassed against me,</u> when they dwelt safely in their land, and none made them afraid. **<u>When I have brought them again from the people, and gathered them out of their enemies'</u>** <u>lands, and am sanctified in them in the sight of many nations;</u> Then shall they know that I am the LORD their God, <u>which caused them to be led into captivity among the heathen:</u> ...(Ezek. 39:21-28; emphasis added)*

What is the significance or importance, at this time in History that Hebrew Israelites awaken to the fact that they are Hebrew Israelites or Israelites? Why does this matter or have to do with one's spiritual salvation? What does it profit one to awaken to the fact that he or she is a Hebrew Israelite or an Israelite by descent and still be lost in his or her sins? What is the greater gain—to learn that I am a Hebrew Israelite or Israelite or to have my sins forgiven? For the Hebrew Israelite, *both* are important in the plan that God has designated for us. Else, why would Jesus/Yehoshua command the disciples to even go to the "Lost Sheep" of Israel with the gospel message of the Kingdom? They were not *lost* to the fact that they were Jews at that time. They knew they were Jews and more than likely were keepers of the Torah. They were *lost* to the fact that the Messiah had come and had given them the *key* into the entrance of the Kingdom— Himself. And what exactly *is* the plan that God designated for the Hebrew Israelites and *its significance* in the end-time? First of all, God Chose Israel to be a Holy Nation and an example to all the other nations through which He would and did send the Messiah, Jesus/Yehoshua, the Savior of the world. Second, the casting away of Israel was done in order that the rest of the World or Gentiles might be reconciled to the Most High God (Rom. 11:11-12, 15). Thirdly the Lord's Second Coming and our own physical deliverance from our present-day captivity as a people seem to be predicated on a massive awakening of the Hebrew Israelites in the end-time followed by a collective repentance and a return unto the Most High as reflected in Deut. 30:1-3, Lev. 26:40-42 and 1 Kings 8:46-51. See scriptures below:

> *And it shall come to pass, when all these things are come upon thee, the blessing and the curse, which I have set before thee, and thou shalt call them to mind among all the nations,*

[207]

*whither the LORD thy God hath driven thee, And shalt **return** unto the LORD thy God, and shalt obey his voice according to all that I command thee this day, thou and thy children, with all thine heart, and with all thy soul;* That **THEN** the LORD thy God WILL **TURN THY CAPTIVITY**, *and have compassion upon thee,* **and WILL RETURN** *and gather thee from all the nations, whither the LORD thy God hath scattered thee.* (Deut. 30:1-3)

If they shall confess their iniquity, and the iniquity of their fathers, with their trespass which they trespassed against me, and that also they have walked contrary unto me; And that I also have walked contrary unto them, and have brought them into the land of their enemies; if then their uncircumcised hearts be humbled, and they then accept of the punishment of their iniquity: **THEN** *will I remember my covenant with Jacob, and also my covenant with Isaac, and also my covenant with Abraham will I remember; and I will remember the land.* (Lev. 26:40-42; emphasis added)

*If they sin against thee, (for there is no man that sinneth not), and thou be angry with them, and deliver them to the enemy, so that they carry them away captives unto the land of the enemy, far or near; Yet if they **shall bethink** themselves in the land whither they were carried captives, **and repent**, and **make supplication unto thee in the land of them that carried them captives**, saying, We have sinned, and have done perversely, we have committed wickedness; **And so return unto thee** with all their heart, and with all their*

[208]

*soul, **in the land of their enemies, which led them away captive**, and pray unto thee toward their land, which thou gavest unto their fathers, the city which thou hast chosen, and the house which I have built for thy name: **THEN** hear thou their prayer and their supplication in heaven thy dwelling place, **and maintain their cause**, And forgive thy people that have sinned against thee, and all their transgressions wherein they have transgressed against thee, and give them compassion before them who carried them captive, that they may have compassion on them: For they be thy people, and thine inheritance, which thou broughtest forth out of Egypt, from the midst of the furnace of iron.* (1 Kings 8:46-51; emphasis added)

In the mouths of two or three witnesses shall every word be established. (2 Cor. 13:1)

Hebrew Israelites, it is time to AWAKEN and do what the Most High God will have us do as a People in these last days—SEEK **HIM** ABOVE ALL ELSE! To the young generation of Hebrew Israelites **in particular**, I say, YOU MUST AWAKEN and SEEK the LORD YOUR GOD with all your heart, with all your mind and with all your soul. TRUST in *Him and the Messiah alone.* Stand strong in the confidence of **His** Delivering, Redeeming, and Conquering Power. When the birth pains begin and heavy persecution befalls God's People unlike never before, keep Psalm 121 forever in the forefront of your minds and hearts. Lift up your eyes unto the hills from whence cometh **our** help and know that our help comes

[209]

from the Lord. "**He** *will not suffer thy foot to be moved; he that keepeth thee will not slumber.* **Behold,** *he that keepeth* **Israel** *shall neither slumber nor sleep…*" However, **we must** do whatever RETURNING unto Him entails and seek Him for this answer.

Finally, **in the end**, this is not a *race* thing. It is a GOD thing. It is what He has declared He would do in the EARTH and HOW He chooses to do it. World History is INDEED HIS STORY. Therefore, since it is HIS story, **HE** gets to write the script—NOT US. The World is in fact a stage—HIS stage. We are all members of HIS CAST performing a role that He has orchestrated *and assigned us.* No role is insignificant. Everyone's part is important. How well we execute our role is dependent on how willing we are to listen, learn from, and follow the DIRECTOR'S lead. If you happen not to like the play, the storyline or the role that you have been assigned, guess what? YOU DO NOT get to REWRITE the SCRIPT according to YOUR LIKING. HIS is NOT a "ME and MY WAY" PRODUCTION. Either you perform the part or role**, *according to script*,** or you can exit, step aside or perhaps forfeit it to an eagerly awaiting understudy. In any case, with or without you, and with or without your approval, HIS PRODUCTION WILL GO ON, <u>AS WRITTEN</u>. HIS WILL SHALL BE DONE, EXACTLY AND WITHOUT FAIL to… THE END!

Shalom.

Yet now hear,

O Jacob my servant; and Israel, whom I have chosen:

Thus saith the LORD that made thee,

and formed thee from the womb, which will help thee;

Fear not, O Jacob, my servant; and thou, Jeshurun,

whom I have chosen. For I will pour water upon him

that is thirsty, and floods upon the dry ground:

I will pour my spirit upon thy seed, and my blessing

upon thine offspring: And they shall spring up as among

the grass, as willows by the water courses.

One shall say, I am the LORD's;

and another shall call himself by the name of Jacob;

and another shall subscribe with his hand unto the

LORD,

and surname himself by the name of Israel.

Thus saith the LORD the King of Israel,

and his redeemer the LORD of hosts;

I am the first, and I am the last;

and beside me there is no God.

(Isaiah 44:1-6)

Stand Strong, Israel. Our Deliverance is NIGH!

Works Cited

"A Brief History of the Terms for Jew." *Jewish Almanac,* 1980, p 3.

Abolitionist. "A Western Misrepresentation of the Jews." *TimBookTu,* 1999, www.timbooktu.com/horton/misrep.html, Accessed 29 Sept. 2015.

Alaezi, Omwukwe Prof. "Jewish Origin of the Ibos, Perspectives from History and Divine Revelation." *IBOS: Hebrew Exiles from Israel Amazing Facts & Revelations,* YAH Publish LLC, 2012, ch. 7, p.54.

Anderson, William C. *The Dictionary of Law,* T.H. Flood and Company,1889. ia800201.us.archive.org/29/items/cu319240228 36534/cu31924022836534.pdf.,10 Aug 2016.

Anthony, Richard. "Should we call ourselves a Christian?" *Devoted to Truth,* 1 Feb.2005, www.ecclesia.org/truth/christian.html, Accessed 15 Oct. 2015.

Anthony, Richard. "The Power of Words: The Words of His Kingdom and the Words of the World Compared." *Devoted to Truth,* 1 Feb.2005, www.ecclesia.org/truth/words.html, Accessed 1 June 2016.

"Apocrypha." *King James Bible online,*
www.kingjamesbibleonline.org/Apocrypha-
Books/, Accessed 7 Oct. 2015.

"Bantu" *Wiktionary,*
https://en.wiktionary.org/wiki/Bantu, 24 Nov.
2015, Accessed 20 Dec. 2016. Used under
Creative Commons Attribution ShareAlike
License.

Bard, Mitchell G. "Nigeria." *Jewish Virtual
Library, 2015,*
www.jewishvirtullibrary.org/jsource/vjw/Nigeri
a.html, Accessed 10 Oct. 2015.

"Byzantine Iconoclasm" Wikipedia the free
encyclopedia 5 May 2017en.wikipedia.org/wiki
/Byzantine_ Iconoclasm.

"Bible Scribes, The."
www.bibleprobe.org/bibauth.html, Accessed 13
Aug. 2016.

"Ceremonial Law, The." *CeremonialLaw.com.,*
2007, www.ceremoniallaw.com/index.html,
Accessed 5 Nov. 2015.

Chambers, Douglas B. *Murder at Montpelier: Igbo
Africans in Virginia.* UP of Mississippi, 1 Mar.
2005, pp. 23, 30-31.

Charles, R.H. tr. *The Book of Enoch.* Introduction
by O. E. Oesterley, DD. Society for Promoting
Christian Knowledge, London, 1917, *Sacred-
texts.* Scanned at sacred-texts.com, June 2004,

[213]

www.sacred-texts.com/bib/boe/boe012.htm,
Accessed 30 Aug. 2016.

Charles, R.H. tr. *The Book of Jubilees.* Introduction
by O. E. Oesterley, DD.Society for Promoting
Christian Knowledge, London 1917, *Sacred-
texts.* Scanned at sacred-texts.com, June 2004,
www.sacred-texts.com/bib/boe/boe012.htm,
Accessed 10 October. 2015.

"Chazars [Khazars]." *The Jewish Encyclopedia,* vol.
4, 1901, Funk & Wagnalls, *Studylight.org,*
Studylight.org, 2002-2015,
www.studylight.org/encyclopedias/tje/view.cgi?
n=4278, Accessed 9 Aug. 2015.

Childress, Clenard Jr. *Blackgenocide.org.*, 2012,
www.blackgenocide.org/black.htm., Accessed 5
Oct. 2015.

"Christmas." Relation to concurrent celebrations,
Wikipedia, the free encyclopedia,
wikipedia.org/wiki/Christmas, 24 June 2016,
Accessed 1 July 2016. Used under Creative
Commons Attribution ShareAlike License.

"Christianity in the 2nd century." *Wikipedia, free
encyclopedia,* 2 May 2016,
wikipedia.org/wiki/Christianity_in_the_2nd_cen
tury, Accessed 16 July 2016. Used under
Creative Commons Attribution ShareAlike
License.

Collins, Martin, "Syncretismas!" Forerunner Commentary, Dec 1995, Bible verses about Christmas Tree, *Bible Tools,* Church of the Great God, 1992- 2016, www.bibletools.org/index.cfm/fuseaction/Topic al.show/RTD/CGG/ID/504/Christmas-Tree.htm.. http://cgg.org, Accessed 22 Dec. 2016.

Davies, Kenneth J. "Who are God's Chosen People?" *Beyond the Endtimes*, Grace Ministries, 2003-2004, http://beyondtheendtimes.com/writing/articles/k _davies/who_are.html, Accessed 1 July 2016.

Davis, Craig. "Witness of the Early Church Father." *Dating the New Testament,* www.datingthenewtestament.com/links.htm, Accessed 1Nov. 2015.

Encyclopedia American, International ed., vols. 30, Grolier, 1985.

"1 Esdras." *New World Encyclopedi*a, 3 Oct. 2013, 14:42 UTC, www.newworldencyclopedia.org/p/index.php?ti tle=1_Esdras&oldid=974409, Accessed 11 Nov. 2015. Used under Creative Commons Attribution ShareAlike License.

"2 Esdras." *Wikipedia, free encyclopedia,* 11 Oct. 2016, https://en.wikipedia.org/wiki/2_Esdras, Accessed 20 Dec. 2016. Used under Creative Commons Attribution ShareAlike License.

"False Image of Christ = Idolatry." *WATCHMAN REPORTS.com*, watchmanreports.com/m/articles/view/False-Image-of-Christ-Idolatry, Accessed 15 Oct. 2015.

"Foreign Relations of the United States," *Office of the Historian"*, vol. E-5, Part 1, Doc 25, Documents on Sub-Saharan Africa 1969-1972, p 2.[3], https://history.state.gov/historicaldocuments/frus1969-76ve05p1/d25-01.

Geiermann, Peter C., SS. R. *Convert's Catechism of Catholic Doctrine,* 1977 ed., Tan Books & Publisher, p. 50.

Freedman, Benjamin. *Facts are Facts.* Bridger House Publishers Inc., 6 Mar. 2009.

Gill, John. "John Gill's Exposition of the Whole Bible." *Studylight.Org.,* Studylight.org, 2001-2016, www.studylight.org, Accessed Aug-Dec 2015.

"Hebrew Roots/Neglected Commandments /Idolatry/Christmas." *Wikbooks,* 7 July 2009, wikibooks.org/wiki/Hebrew_Roots/Neglected_Commandments/Idolatry/Christmas, Accessed 14 July 2016. Used under Creative Commons Attribution ShareAlike License.

Holy Bible, King James Version, *BibleGateway*.
www.biblegateway.com/, Accessed 1 June
2015-15 May 2016.

"Igbo People." *Wikipedia, the free encyclopedia*,
15 Nov. 2015, wikipedia.org/wiki/Igbopeople,
Accessed 28 Nov. 2015, Used under Creative
Commons Attribution ShareAlike License.

"Igbo People in the Atlantic Slave Trade."
Wikipedia, the free encyclopedia, 18 Dec 2015,
en.wikipedia.org/wiki/Igbo_people_in_the_Atla
ntic_slave_trade, Accessed 28 Dec. 2015. Used
under Creative Commons Attribution
ShareAlike License.

"Images of the True Israelites - B'Nai Zaqen"
http://sarabe3.tripod.com/israeliteimages.html.
Accessed 28 Nov. 2015.

"Is Jesus a Myth?" *Gotquestions.com*, Got Question
Ministries, 2002-2016,
www.gotquestions.org/Jesus-myth.html,
Accessed 18 July 2016.

"Jacob." *Wikipedia, the free encyclopedia*, 27 June
2016, https://en.wikipedia.org/wiki/Jacob,
Accessed 28 June 2016. Used under Creative
Commons Attribution ShareAlike License.

",Jospeth (patriach)." *Wikipedia, the free
encyclopedia*, 28 June 2016,
wikipedia.org/wiki/Joseph_(patriarch),

Accessed 29 June 2016. Used under Creative
Commons Attribution ShareAlike License.

Kelly, J.N.D. *Early Christian Doctrines-Revised.*
HarperOne Imprint of Harper Collins
Publishers, 1978, pp. 53-56.

Kelly, Russell. "UNCONDITIONAL PROMISES
TO ISRAEL" 2 Oct. 2015, www.tithing-
russkelly.com/theology/id13.html, Accessed 9
Nov. 2015.

"Kumbaya." *Wikipedia, the free encyclopedia,* 21
Nov. 2015, wikipedia.org/wiki/Kumbaya,
Accessed 29 Nov. 2015. Used under Creative
Commons Attribution ShareAlike License.

Lang, Stephen J. *Everyday Biblical Literacy: The
Essential Guide to Biblical and Allusions in Art,
Literature and Life.* Writer's Digest Books, 27
Feb. 2007, p. 163.
books.google.com/books?id=VqrT7sz9Xb0C&p
g=PP9&lpg=PP9&dq=Lang,+Stephen+J.+Every
day+Biblical+Literacy:++The+Essential+Guide
+to+Biblical+and+Allusions, Accessed 18 July
2016.

Lange, Dierk. "Origin of the Yoruba and the 'Lost
Tribes of Israel.'" *Anthropos,* 106.2011, pp.
579-595.

Larue, Gerald A. "Ancient Jewish History: Who
were the Hebrews?" *Jewish Virtual Library,* 22
Oct. 2015,

www.jewishvirtuallibrary.org/jsource/History/h
ebrews.html, Accessed 20 Dec. 2015.

Lilienthal, Alfred M. *The Zionist Connection II,*
"What Price Peace?" Veritas Publishing
Company PTY Ltd, 1983, pp. 759-768

Locker, Herbert, Sr. Ed . *Illustrated Dictionary of
the Bible,* consulting editors: F. F Bruce, R.K.
Harrison. Thomas Nelson Publisher, 1986,
p.392.

Luginbill, Dr. Robert. "What does the name
'Christian' mean?" *ICHTHYS Bible Study for
Spiritual Growth,* ichthys.com/mail-the-name-
Christian.html, Accessed 14 July 2016.

Lynch, Willie."Full text of Willie Lynch Letter
1712."
archive.org/stream/WillieLynchLetter1712/the_
willie_lynch_letter_the_making_of_a_slave_17
12_djvu.txt, Accessed 23 Oct. 2015.

"1 Maccabees." Wikipedia, the free encyclopedia,
25 July 2016,
en.wikipedia.org/wiki/1_Maccabees, Accessed
18 Aug. 2016. Used under Creative Commons
Attribution ShareAlike License.

MacDonald, William. *Believer's Bible
Commentary.* Edited by Art Farstard, Thomas
Nelson Publishers, 1980, 1983, 1985, 1986,
1990, pp. 1110.1898.

"Merneptah Stele." *Wikipedia, the free encyclopedia,* wikipedia.org/wiki/Merneptah_Stele, Accessed 26 Oct. 2015. Used under Creative Commons Attribution ShareAlike License.

"More Curses & Prophesies." *Angelfire.com,* www.angelfire.com/ill/hebrewisrael/printpages/ morecurses.html, Accessed 10 Oct. 2015.

Nasi, Aria. "The Bantu Branch of 'Africans' are Hebrew Israelites, PART II of II." *Aria Nasi Research,* Aria Nasi Research, 2014-2015, arianasiresearch.wordpress.com/2015/02/14/the-bantu-branch-of-africans-are-hebrew-israelites-part-ii-of-ii/, Accessed 28 Sept. 2015.

Naugle, David. "Jesus Christ and the Kingdom of God." *Kingdom Living (13) The Christian Worldview Journal,* 26 Apr. 2010, www.colsoncenter.org/the-center/columns/indepth/15062-jesus-christ-and-the-kingdom-of-god, Accessed 15 Nov. 2015.

New World Encyclopedia Contributors. "Bantu." *New World Encyclopedia,* 11 May 2015, 14:40 UTC, www.newworldencyclopedia.org/p/index.php?ti tle=Bantu&oldid=995896, Accessed 10 Oct. 2015, Used under Creative Commons Attribution ShareAlike License.

"Origin of Christmas, The," Hebrew Roots/Neglected Commandments/Idolatry/

Christmas *Wikibooks,*
https://en.wikibooks.org/wiki/Hebrew_Roots/Ne
glected_Commandments/Idolatry/Christmas, 7
July, 2009. Used under Creative Commons
Attribution ShareAlike License.

"Ouidah." *Wikipedia, the free encyclopedia*
https://fr.wikipedia.org/wiki/Ouidah, 12 Apr.
2016, Accessed 28 Dec, 2016. Used under
Creative Commons Attribution ShareAlike
License.

Pedrin, Michael. "Question 31: In John 4:22, Jesus
Said, "salvation is of the Jews, Then where do
we stand?" *Clear Bible Answers,*
clearbibleanswers.org/questionsanswers/212-in-
john-422-jesus-said salvation-is-of-the-jews-
then-where-do-we-stand.html, 3 Sept. 2008,
Accessed 11 Feb 2016.

"Portal:Igbo." *Wikipedia, the free encyclopedia,* 21
August 2015, en.wikipedia.org/wiki/Portal:Igbo,
Accessed 5 May 2016. Used under Creative
Commons Attribution ShareAlike License

"Prayer of Azariah." *The King James Bible online,*
2015,www.kingjamesbibleonline.org/Prayer-of-
Azariah-Chapter-1/, ch. 1:1-3, 66-68, Accessed
1 Nov. 2015.

"Prayer of Azariah and Song of the Three Holy
Children, The." *Wikipedia, the free
encyclopedia,* 2 Apr. 2016,
wikipedia.org/wiki/The_Prayer_of_Azariah_and

_Song_of_the_Three_Holy_Children, Accessed 29 July 2016. Used under Creative Commons Attribution ShareAlike License.

"Prayer of Manasseh." *The King James Version online*, 2015, www.kingjamesbibleonline.org/Prayer-of-Manasseh-Chapter-1/. ch. 1, Accessed 29 Oct. 2015.

Publisher's Preface. "The Apocrypha in the King James Version." *The Holy Bible, King James Version*, Ed. 1611, Hendrickson Publishers Marketing, LLC., 2010, p.4.

Ragsdale, Justin J. "Black Babies Used as Alligator Bait... Lest we forget 4 of 4." 9 Sept. 2009, www.youtube,com/watch?v=YMHO8zyTPyU, Accessed 15 Nov. 2015.

"Robert Taylor (Radical)" *Wikipedia, the free encyclopedia*, 2 May, 2015, wikipedia.org/wiki/Robert_Taylor_(Radical), Accessed 8 Oct. 2015. Used under Creative Commons Attribution ShareAlike License.

"Sabbath." (Seventh -day versus First- day) *Wikipedia, the free encyclopedia,* 7 Nov. 2015, wikipedia.org/wiki/Sabbath, Accessed 11 Nov. 2015. Used under Creative Commons Attribution ShareAlike License.

"Serapis vs Jesus." *Tekton Apologetics*, Tekton Apologetic Ministries,

www.tektonics.org/copycat/serapis.php,
Accessed 12 July 2016.

"Statistics of incarcerated African American
males." *Wikipedia, the free encyclopedia*, June
29, 2015,
wikipedia.org/wiki/Statistics_of_incarcerated_A
frican-American_males, Accessed 15 Sept.
2015. Used under Creative Commons
Attribution ShareAlike License.

Thomsen, Emily. " Catholic Church Admits They
Made the Change." *Sabbath Truth, 2003,*
www.sabbathtruth.com/free-resources/article-
library/id/916/catholic-church-admits-they-
made-the-change, Accessed 5 Oct. 2015.

Trans-Atlantic Slave Trade Data, Emory
University, 2013, GPL3 ver. 1.2
slavevoyages.org/, Accessed 10 June; 29 Nov
2015.

Treybig, David. " 'The Kingdom of God is Within
You'—What Did Christ Mean?" *Life, Hope &
Truth,* Church of God, A Worldwide
Association, INC., 2015,
/lifehopeandtruth.com/prophecy/kingdom-of-
god/the-kingdom-of-god-is-within-you/,
Accessed 11 Nov. 2015.

Treybig, David, "Why did God Choose Israel?"
Life, Hope & Truth, Church of God, A
Worldwide Association, INC., 2015,
/lifehopeandtruth.com/prophecy/12-tribes-of-

israel/why-did-god-choose-israel/Accessed 10 Nov. 2015.

Ware, Bruce. "What criteria were used to determine the canon of Scripture?" *BiblicalTraining*, 10 July 2012, www.biblicaltraining.org/blog/curious-christian/7-10-2012/what-criteria-were-used-determine-canon-scripture, Accessed 31 Oct. 2015.

"What are the times of the Gentiles?" *GotQuestions.org,*. Got Questions Ministries, 2002-2015, www.gotquestions.org/times-of-the-Gentiles.html, Accessed 15 Oct. 2015.

"What does it mean that the church has been grafted in Israel's Palace?" *GotQuestions.org.,* Got Questions Ministries, 2002-2015, www.gotquestions.org/times-of-the-Gentiles.html, Accessed 15 Oct. 2015.

Whiston, William A.M. translator, *Josephus: The Complete Works*, Thomas Nelson Publishers, 1998, pp. 888-895.

"Who Was Really Born on December 25?" *Gilead Institute of America*, The Gilead Institute of America, 2016, www.gilead.net/study/holidays/christmasorigin2.html, Accessed 2 July 2016.

"Why did God choose Israel to be His chosen people?" *GotQuestions.org,*.Got Questions Ministries, 2002-2015, www.gotquestions.org/times-of-the-Gentiles.html, Accessed 11 Nov. 2015.

"Why Don't People Understand the Kingdom of God?" *Beyond Today.* United Church of God, 1995-2016, www.ucg.org/bible-study-tools/booklets/the-gospel-of-the-kingdom/why dont-people-understand-the-kingdom-of-god, Accessed 28 July 2016.

Windsor, Rudolph R. *From Babylon to Timbuktu: A History of the Ancient Black Races Including the Black Hebrews.* Windsor Golden Series, 1969-2003, pp. 84, 87.

Wisdom of Solomon. *The Official King James Version online.* 2015, www.kingjamesbibleonline.org/Wisdom-of-Solomon-Chapter-4/, .Accessed 3 Nov. 2015.

"Yeshua." *Wikipedia, the free encyclopedia,* 21 June 2016, wikipedia.org/wiki/Yeshua, Accessed 28 June 2016. Used under Creative Commons Attribution ShareAlike License.

Young, Douglas, G. *Young's Bible Dictionary.* Tyndale Desktop Reference Series, Tyndale House Publishers, INC., 2007, pp. 255-56.

"Yule." *Wikipedia, the free encyclopedia,* wikipedia.org/wiki/Yule, 27 June 2016. Accessed 8 July 2016. Used under Creative Commons Attribution ShareAlike License.

Suggested Resources

Chapter I

DNA and the Jewish Bloodline

"DNA Test Confirming Khazaran/Ashkenazi Jews Are Not the Blood Descendants of Hebrew Israelites," (August 2015), www.youtube.com/watch?v=fypCbRKMDUM.

Eran. Elhaik. "The Missing Link of Jewish European Ancestry: Contrasting the Rhineland and the Khazarian Hypotheses". *Genome Biology and Evolution*, 2012 vol. 5, iss.1, pp 61-74, gbe.oxfordjournals.org/content/5/1/61.full?sid=dcd627ca-e4fa-455c-a277-0cb54b60632c

Fake Jews and the Coming Destruction of Israel search.yahoo.com/search?fr=mcafee&type=A01 1US0&p=Watch+LaterFake+Jews+And+The+C oming+Destruction+Of+Israel

Jack Otto, Lecturer. "Forbidden Knowledge History of the Khazar Empire." Lecture, search.yahoo.com/search?fr=mcafee&type=A01 1US0&p=Watch+LaterForbidden+Knowledge+ -+History+of+the+Khazar+Empire+- +Lecture+by+Jack+Otto

Marrs, Texe. *DNA Science and the Jewish Bloodline.* RiverCrest Publisher, 2013 amazon.com/dp/B00DUHSHEG/ref=rdr_kindle _ext_tmb#nav-subnav.

"The JEWS are BLACK pt.2 The LEMBA migration from JERUSALEM 70 AD." www.youtube.com/watch?v=RYrQvm_llBY

WJC (World Jewish Congress). "Lemba tribe in southern Africa has Jewish roots, genetic tests reveal." 8 Mar. 2010, World Jewish Congress, 2016, www.worldjewishcongress.org/en/news/lemba-tribe-in-southern-africa-has-jewish-roots-genetic-tests-reveal. Accessed 5 July 2016.

JTA. "African tribe descended from Jews, DNA tests show," *The Jerusalem Post, 3/8/2010,* http://www.jpost.com/Jewish-World/Jewish-News/African-tribe-descended-from-Jews-DNA-tests-show. Accessed 29 June 2016.

Thomas, Mark G. et al. "Y Chromosomes Traveling South: The Cohen Modal Haplotype and the Origins of the Lemba—the 'Black Jews' of Southern Africa." *The American Journal of Human Genetics.* vol. 59, 1996, Published online 2000 Feb 11. doi: 10.1086/302749, Accessed 13 September 2016.

"Digging For the Truth —The Lost Tribe of Israel." www.youtube.com/watch?v=B2sSaVFXjLA

Additional Resources on the Ashkenazi Jews

The Encyclopedia Judaica. vol. 10, Keter
Publishing House, Jerusalem, 1971-1972.

The Universal Jewish Encyclopedia. vol. 10, KTAV
Publishing House, Inc.,1969.

The New Encyclopedia Britannica, 15th ed., vol. 6
Encyclopedia Britannica, Inc., 1992, p. 836.

Academic American Encyclopedia. Deluxe Library
ed., vol. 12, 1985, p. 66.

1961 Speech by Benjamin Freedman Transcript
Version,
www.sweetliberty.org/issues/israel/freedman.htm

1961 Speech by Benjamin Freedmam Youtube
audio version—Published 29 Dec. 2013.
www.youtube.com/watch?v=x8OmxI2AYV8.
Accessed 16 May, 2016.

Keostler, Arthur. *The Thirteenth Tribe: The Khazar
Empire and Its Heritage* Random House, 1976,
www.fantompowa.info/koestlerindex.htm

Ancient Hebrew Israelites' Physical Appearance & The True Jews.

Picture of Hebrew Israelites with afros in an ancient Egyptian tomb, www.youtube.com/watch?v=XookxSWjk4w

"Biblical Israelites were Black and Still are Today!" www.youtube.com/watch?v=nWnox4IpC5c

Ashkenazi Jew speaks the truth Black people are 12 Tribes of Israel www.youtube.com/watch?v=-gf6UAIVeJQ

"The TRUE Hebrews defined by Scripture and history. WARNING you will be shocked!!" www.youtube.com/watch?v=bEDfrBBPZzg

Images of true Hebrew Israelites www.youtube.com/watch?v=7i_cUvZRBPk

"Surely our fathers have inherited lies,... (Israelites)." www.youtube.com/watch v=WGv8fs8yfWA. (Jer. 16:19).

"Identity of Israelites Will Shock and Confound the Wicked! (SHORT TAKE)." www.youtube.com/watch?v=-BczMPXcaSA

"White Woman Exposes Who the Real Jews are According to the Bible and History," www.youtube.com/watch?v=_btf_Y_ua98

"Whited Out Documentary: The True Israelites were black, Asians & Native Americans were also black."
www.youtube.com/watch?v=NX0DtMiYxEM.
Aug. 26, 2014- Uploaded by the Watchman Reports.

White Cop Tell the Truth on Why Blacks are being Killed by White Cops.
www.youtube.com/watch?v=uyddRttYRWI

Hebrew Tribes in West Africa

William, Joseph J. *Hebrewism of West Africa, From Nile To Niger With The Jews*. George Allen & Unwin LTD, 1930.

"Hebrew Kingdom of Judah found in West Africa,"
www.youtube.com/watch?v=DSYzSerEYzM.

"Ghana Rising History: Are the Ashantis [Akans] from Ashan in Israel?"
ghanarising.blogspot.com/2013/03/history-are-ashantis-akans-from-ashan.html

European Jews and the Slave Trade

Sertima Van, Ivan. *African Presence in Early Europe*. Transaction Publishers, 1 Jan 1987.

Journal of African Civilizations, Nov. 1985,
Vol. 7, No. 2.

Donnan, Elizabeth, *Documents Illustrative of the
History of the Slave Trade to America.* Carnegie
Institution of Washington, 1932.

Historical Research Department of NOI. *The Secret
Relationship Between Blacks and Jews.* Nation
of Islam; 2nd ed. 12 Aug. 2010.

Black Babies as Alligator Bait

"Alligator Bait." *Jim Crow Museum of Racist
Memorabilia,* Ferris State University and
Miami.
www.ferris.edu/htmls/news/jimcrow/question/m
ay13/index.htm

Strouse, Chuck. "Black Babies Used as Alligator
Bait in Florida." *Miami New Times, 3* F., 2014.

The Apocrypha

Stewart, Don. "Why Does the Roman Catholic
Church Accept the Books of the Old Testament
Apocrypha as Holy Scripture?" *Blue Letter
Bible.* 24 Apr, 2007.

www.blueletterbible.org//faq/don_stewart/don_s
tewart_394.cfm. Accessed 11 Aug. 2016.

"Black Biblical Icons & White-Washing Biblical
Icons," Ivanov, Vladimir. *Russian Icons.*
Rizzoli; 1st ed., Nov 15, 1990.

Black Biblical Icons & White Washing Biblical Icon

Ivanov, Vladimir. *Russian Icons.* Rizzoli; 1st ed.,
Nov 15, 1990.

Russian Icons
https://www.youtube.com/watch?v=uWBtxGM
z1CE

Russian Icons: Paintings Of Israelites
https://www.youtube.com/watch?v=cU4eTrHqp
4g

Ancient Man and His First Civilizations How did
Jesus and the Hebrews become WHITE?
http://realhistoryww.com/world_history/ancient/
Misc/Jesus/Jesus.htm

Cesare Borgia

"FAKE JESUS CHRIST Cesare Borgia Son of Pope Alexander VI." www.youtube.com/watch?v=6jcZ17HrnJU.

Marion, Johnson, *The Borgia*, Penguin Books, March 26 2002.

Chapter 2

Sabbath Change

Scheifler, Michael. "Exactly Which Pope Changed the Sabbath to Sunday? A Challenge to Adventist Answered." *Michael Scheiflier's Bible Light Homepage*, biblelight.net/sylvester-1.htm. Accessed 1 Aug. 2016.

Pagan Roots of Christmas

Meyer, David J. "The True Meaning of Christ-Mass" *Last Trumpet Ministries International*. www.lasttrumpetministries.org/tracts/tract4.html. Accessed 15 Oct. 2015.

"Tracing the Roots of Christmas." *The (Ephesus) Church of God*, 1980-2017, www.thevisionofall.org/TracingtheRootsofChristmas.html. Accessed 9 Nov. 2015.